CONTRACTOR'S
BLUEPRINT

Getting CONTROL of Your Business, to GROW Your Business and Achieve Personal & Financial FREEDOM

JIM JOHNSON

HOLON
PUBLISHING

www.Holon.co

ISBN#: 978-1- 955342-48-3 (Hardback)
ISBN#: 978-1- 955342-49-0 (Paperback)
ISBN#: 978-1- 955342-45-2 (eBook)

Published by:

Holon Publishing & Collective Press
A Storytelling Company
www.Holon.co

Work ON It, Not IN It!

Introduction

This book is a guide to uncovering the strategies and tactics that help contractors and entrepreneurs immediately create a shift and start to work ON their business instead of IN their business. Most contractors start a business based on their craftsmanship abilities, sales skills, or simply because they believe they can do it better than who they are working for. Unfortunately, this positions them as an employee, and not just any employee but the key employee. By becoming the key employee, they are forced to wear a multitude of hats. The owner's hat, the sales leader's hat, the production leader's hat, the administrative leader's hat, the finance leader's hat, and many more. They get caught in the trap of working for their business instead of it working for them. Most never escape the trap and are in a constant state of frustration, always searching for the secret to leading a thriving business. Why? It doesn't have to be this way. Others have done it and so can you with the *Contractor's Blueprint*. I wish someone had written this guide when we were taking our contracting business from zero to $5 million in it's very first year, to over $20+ million in annual revenue each year after that. It would have been easier, faster, and so much less stressful. I would have avoided tons of mistakes and saved a lot of time that I could have spent with my family and friends. I hope to save you that pain with the *Contractor's Blueprint*.

This is the first step-by-step guide that is proven to turn six-figure contractors into seven-figure contractors, and seven-figure contractors into eight-figure contractors. The proof is in the over 400 contractors who have achieved 7 and 8 figure businesses after following the *Contractor's Blueprint* with our guided coaching.

The strategies shared in this book will give you the blueprint to grow and scale your business in a way you've always known you were capable of, but never knew how. Many self-made entrepreneurs are swimming in chaos, have sleepless nights, are too busy reacting to be proactive, work seemingly endless hours, and are wearing all the "hats." The reason for this is because they're working for their business, rather than their business working for them. If you don't know how to position yourself as an owner instead of an employee of your business, it will leave you in a never-ending cycle of work—so much so that you won't find the time to work on it. Are you ready to create the time to work on your business?

At my organization, Contractor Coach PRO, our purpose is "Empowering People to Believe!" by coaching contractors from around the world.

After 8 years of this work, *we discovered that there is a very distinct set of strategies, when executed in the correct order,* that leads to tremendous scalability—and more importantly—growth and overall success of a business. In our industry, 70-80% of contractors fail within the first three years. Our 100% client success rate of staying in business beyond those three years and thriving speaks for itself. It is my hope that this book can help even more contractors believe in their work by developing the strategies and tactics they need to make their dreams achievable.

When it comes to these strategies and tactics, even the most basic concepts can apply to most businesses. However, for the purposes of this book and the passion I have for the home services contractor, they were written specifically for you.

Although a lot has been written about these strategies, they tend to neglect the order.

So, while we might have the tools we need to succeed, we don't understand how to use them and when. To the best of my knowledge, there isn't a book on the fundamental strategies and tactics needed to succeed as a contractor, in the correct order, that needs to be considered when growing and scaling a business and why that order is so important. This was an incredible epiphany for me and our team, and I hope it will be for you as well. I believe this is a huge factor in the success or failure of new businesses across the world. It's like doing a math equation out of order; your answer is doomed to be wrong. This is why I titled my book *Contractor's Blueprint*. It is a detailed, chronological plan for your business. If you follow these steps to completion, you will have one hell of a business on your hands.

It is important to understand that the strategy alone is not enough to ensure the success of your business. It is the order in which you choose to implement these strategies, and your belief in your company that will ultimately determine the success of your business.

Each of our businesses exist in their own time and place. There are varying degrees of "battles" that each will need to win to ultimately have our business working for us, instead of us for it. The strategies and tactics you execute in your specific situation will weigh heavily on the legacy you leave behind as a leader.

Choose wisely...

.

Contents

ture of your organization, how that organization communicates, and how you will handle HR early on makes decision making and accountability in the future a no brainer.

Know Your Numbers and How to Manage Them
After leadership, an understanding of finance and your cash flow are the most common reasons a contractor fails. Get a handle on your numbers to make great decisions about your finances without the guessing.

Setting a Standard of Excellence
If it can be measured it can be improved. Find your "North Star Metric" and what you should be measuring. Use that knowledge to keep everyone accountable to the expectations set from day one. Also, learn how to set standards for sales productivity, commissions, and activity that will drive revenue and profit through the roof.

Foreword
Written by Zac Kerr

Home service contractors ensure that as individuals and families we are safe, comfortable, and able to live our best lives by providing incredibly important services to our homes and properties.

The trade services that keep our lives running are indeed some of the most valuable and important services we can access in our communities. And behind every commercial contractor and trades services business are individuals and families who are exchanging their important contribution to our community and building their own dream and reality. These are individuals and families pursuing careers, economic freedom, personal prosperity, and the pride of growing and maintaining a successful business. There is something special about a business owner or founder who seeks to improve their business and livelihood by leveling up their capabilities so they can create more of whatever it is that they desire. As part of the human condition, we all desire increase and advancement. In the trades businesses, there can be a real challenge for solo founders to grow their business to a point of scale that they achieve the level of freedom from their business that allows them to be more intentional with their time and personal priorities. People weren't destined to only work in this life, we were destined for so much more. In order to achieve the best version of our lives and do what we are really destined to do, we have to learn to *work on* what we are doing and not just *work inside of* what we are doing. To me, the title of this book surfaces the idea of metacognition, which is thinking about how we think. Metacognition is "cognition about cognition," "thinking about thinking," "knowing about knowing," becoming "aware of one's awareness," and higher-order thinking skills. The term comes from the root word *meta*, meaning "beyond," or "on top of." Metacognition can take many forms, and it includes knowledge about when and how to use particular strategies for learning or problem-solving.

I've been around the field services businesses for nearly two decades, but especially the last 7 years. As Co-founder at SalesRabbit, and industry contributor, I have had the honor to be alongside thousands of service businesses learning and working with founders and leaders as they work on their businesses and lives. In our modern-day, business progress means personal progress, and personal progress manifests results in business progress. Everything is personal, and we should prioritize as such. Behind every great business is a great man or woman who has studied the timeless universal principles of providence and prosperity. How you define greatness in building your trades business is a personal definition, but for me it's so much more than a balance sheet, it's about being the best version of yourself, and doing meaningful life work.

"In the past jobs were about muscles, now they're about brains, but in the future they'll be about the heart."
—Dame Minouche Shafik

I think blending muscles, heart, and brains is the present and future of trades businesses. I can't think of anyone more qualified to take you on a journey to elevate all three attributes than Jim Johnson. Jim's important invitation to all of us is to advance our lives, to go beyond, to be on top of it, and to practice the strategies of "working on it not in it" affording us the freedom to chase our dreams.

Preface

A little over eight years ago, in a moment of prayer, I decided to resign from my position as Director of Sales for a software company for contractors. I've heard many people say God spoke to them and they followed his command. I've prayed an awful lot over my lifetime, and I've yet to hear the "voice of God," but I have had a clear and strong "feeling" that it was time to make a particular decision. Call it "gut instinct," "intuition," "God's Voice," or whatever you will. When I feel it, there is no other option than to listen. One word repeated itself over and over in my head...

"Resign, resign, resign..." So I did.

In the last eight years I have learned more about being a contractor and entrepreneur than in the 44 years prior. I have learned how to learn and understand people, and I have no regrets. I am loving the journey and opportunity to help people achieve their dreams and empower others to find their version of success. Nothing could be more fulfilling to me right now.

With that said, no matter your spiritual persuasion and beliefs, if you're a contractor, this book will be the guide to the strategies and tactics you need to get control of your business and achieve your dreams. We'll get back to those dreams later in the book.

As I was saying, I had a clear and strong feeling that it was time to make a change. The word that kept resonating as I prayed was, "resign." No reason why, just do it. It was the first time

I've ever left one opportunity without knowing exactly what the next was going to be. Talk about faith!

The next day, I wrote my letter of resignation and flew to the headquarters to break the news to our CEO. There was no doubt I needed to do this.

When I handed over my letter to the CEO, it was clear I had caught him off guard. His feelings were apparent in his facial expression as he read the letter. There was a "I can't believe you're doing this" look that said it all. The thing I appreciated most was that he was also concerned about me and how this decision would affect my future.

Why was it such a surprise? Well, if there's anyone that's passionate about the application of software in the contracting industry, it's me. I loved my time there, the people I worked with, the purpose of helping contractors succeed, and all the individuals we helped to do so. I love how software can help us communicate more efficiently, both internally and externally, to provide a better experience for our customers and team. That's what it's all about: better serving one another. To lose the person championing your "why" to an industry with pretty solid results can be a little bit of a shock. To hear that person say they don't know why they are resigning, other than they just know they have to, can be a real shock. To this day it seems surreal.

I assured him and the team that I still believed in the mission; I just wasn't the one that would take them over the finish line. I'd learn later that I (along with a lot of great people) had helped lay the foundation so that the company could grow and scale.

Together we wrote a press release that made it clear the company's software was still the best choice of CRM for home services contractors and that my leaving in no way hindered my belief in the product.

We put it together that day, along with the promise that I would help find my replacement to assist in the next phase of their growth.

I flew home the next day to find that the most important mentor in my life, my grandfather, was on the way to the hospital because (as we would find out later), he had bone cancer. He had been dealing with it for several years without realizing that the extreme pain he was feeling wasn't just what happens as we age after a hard life. That man was able to handle more pain than anyone I have ever met.

My grandfather has more to do with who I've become than any other person in my life. I immediately drove three hours to be with him and my grandmother. For the next five days and four nights, I stayed awake because he was awake and fighting. During that trying time, the press release came out and my phone literally exploded with calls, texts, and emails from dozens of contractors wanting me to be a part of their business.

I simply turned my phone off and focused on my grandparents. I finally understood the need I had felt to resign. I needed some final coaching from my greatest mentor. There was more for me to do, and they needed me there.

I spent every moment I could over the next three months talking and spending time with "Pappy." We talked about trips we'd been on together, the first fish I had caught on a flyrod, when he first met my grandmother and just "knew" she was the one (he always introduced her as his "first wife" with a chuckle), his career in the military, how much he thought of my wife, and most of all about how he had found God late in life. He shared his gratitude for this revelation and his regret for not having had it earlier. We also talked about how different our spiritual views were and the ways in which he disagreed with mine, but that he still loved me and would pray for me.

During these three months, he asked what I would do now that I had resigned. It was the first time I can remember telling him, "I don't know" when asked about my career. I still remember him saying, "Well we better figure it out. I know you're not just going to sit around and do nothing."

When he asked me what I wanted to do, my instant response, without hesitation, was to be a college basketball coach. Once the laughter subsided, he asked if it was basketball or the coaching that gave me energy. For the last 25 years, I have coached everything from kindergarteners to college athletes in baseball and basketball. I had to really stop and think, *was it the sport or was it the coaching?* Then he asked me what I was great at. Again, I instantly responded that I knew this home services contractor thing better than most. Again, laughter followed by a question. Was it being a contractor or was it leading a team to win? I had, after all, helped build one of the largest health and fitness franchises in the country in my former life (before contracting).

Key Point: Up to this point, those are the two most powerful questions I've ever been asked. Who was I, and what gave me joy and fulfillment? I realize now that he knew who I was and who I could be better than I did. He knew because he listened, observed, and helped me to come to the answer on my own. To this day, I am grateful for his wisdom. Those two questions are the first questions we ask all of our clients. I needed to serve others as a coach, and I knew coaching to win would fulfill me.

Over those last three months, we talked about what it would look like to be a business coach for contractors. I'm sure they existed at the time, but I hadn't heard of any. Afterwards, I located a few, but they were more consultants for contractors or general business coaches. Today there are dozens and dozens of coaches in our industry.

We identified there were major differences between consultants and coaches. Consultants wear suits, ties, and/or sports coats. They evaluate a business or situation and develop a course of action for the client to take. They normally charge a huge fee and walk away leaving you with the choice to execute or not.

Coaches, on the other hand, dress a little more casually (90% of the time, I'm in a ball cap, t-shirt, and coaching pants). They develop strategies and tactics—a game plan—based on the right system for the team and their assets. They teach the fundamentals, evaluate the execution of the game plan, reinforce the fundamentals, add skills, and are always striving for perfection. Ideally, they experience a lot of wins. They know their player's strengths and weaknesses and put them in position to win. They encourage and inspire their team to be better every day because they are all working toward the same goal. Again, alignment with who I am and why I exist.

Pappy was the inspiration and wisdom behind our coaching business, Contractor Coach PRO. I wish he were here today to see what we've been able to accomplish. The businesses we've helped grow, the businesses we've helped avoid bankruptcy, the marriages we've saved, the lives we've given purpose, and the leaders we've helped build. Most of all, the impact we've been able to have on an industry. We still have so much to do, but slowly and surely, we are making a difference. At times it seems overwhelming, but I wouldn't change this journey for anything. The really cool part of it all is that it's not about us.

It's about you, the home services contractor and their mentors and coaches. You are the ones doing the hard work to make your dreams come true. We just have the experience and blueprint to get you there more quickly. I couldn't be prouder of our contractors and friends that we have had the opportunity to serve. Through that service, you have made this book possible. You guys ROCK!

Over these past 13 years as the Director of Sales at the software company and now as Head Coach at Contractor Coach PRO, I've had the opportunity to "pull back the curtain" on the operations of over 1,500 contractors. It has been truly amazing to see all the ways they've achieved success as well as struggled. Training our coaches and teaching contractors to work *on* their business rather than *for* it, has given me a unique body of knowledge. We aren't here to coach the Jim Johnson way. We exist to coach you in the best way for you. *Key Point:* In other words, there are no "silver bullet systems," there is only the system you believe in. The one you are willing to pour yourself into—the one that takes hard work. There are so many different ways to do this, and we will help you to find the one that works for you.

The reason I wrote this book is because over these past few years, I've had a bit of an epiphany. Although there are several ways to succeed as a contractor, the same basic blueprint applies to all. We call it the "Contractor's Blueprint." In other words, there are key areas of your business that need tending to. This should be done in a very specific order, and you must have a strategy or you will constantly be in "firefighter" mode. You will always be reacting to fires instead of taking proactive actions to prevent fires from ever happening. This keeps us in a position of always working in our business instead of on it, keeping us from achieving those dreams we had when we started. We end up becoming employees of our business instead of leaders running it. In other words, without these key strategies and the tactics to execute them, done in the order you see in this book, your potential will always be capped. Can you succeed financially? Yes, depending on what that means for you, but is that all you have the potential for? I hope not.

Contractor DNA

Why do you think we use the word "grow" to describe expanding our businesses? Why do some people refer to their business as their "baby"? Why do we care so much about our businesses?

The answer to these questions is that your business is a living, breathing thing that needs constant attention to go from birth, to adolescence, to maturity. If you do it right, you might even leave behind a legacy that outlives you. Sound familiar? It sounds like raising a child, and in many ways that is exactly what you are doing. Just like having children, some parents are more prepared than others. In order for you to understand the responsibility of raising this child, we need to have a little business biology class.

It all starts with you. You have a very particular DNA and personality that you are going to pass along to this business of yours. When you involve partners, you start to multiply that DNA. If they aren't compatible, you run the risk of compromising your business before it is born or during its infancy. Just like Mom and Dad, we have to be on the same page about the strategies and tactics we will use to "raise this child" to be successful.

Picture the human double DNA helix you learned about in biology, you have two backbone strands connected by a sequence of components that make up your unique DNA. Like human DNA, there are two backbones, if you will, of a Contractor's DNA. The Foundational Backbone and Operational Backbone. The Foundational Backbone is exactly what it sounds like: your business' foundation. It is the brain, nervous system, and musculoskeletal foundation of your business. The Foundational Backbone is made up of your Leadership, Culture, Process, Organization & Human Resources, Numbers & Finance, and Accountability. This book will focus on the Foundational Backbone of your business and how that impacts the Operational Backbone. The Operational Backbone is what people see on the outside; it is based on the stimulus to and strength of the Foundational Backbone. This is the skin, hair, eye color and overall beauty or ugliness of your offspring. If you have ever heard the old saying, "you can put lipstick on a pig, but it's still a pig," then you can understand what a company that looks good on the outside is dealing with internally when they go out of business. They weren't healthy on the inside. The Operational Backbone of your business is Technology, Marketing, Sales, Production, Training, Recruiting Hiring & Onboarding. Everything you do foundationally will determine the success of how you will perform operationally. If you use the *Contractor's Blueprint*, not only will your business be beautiful on the outside, but it will be healthy on the inside.

Like any other living thing, if a piece of your DNA is out of sync, you're in for a lot of issues. Also like traditional DNA, if yours is out of order, you're going to have major problems.

This Contractor DNA sequence has been the single biggest tool of our coaching practice. *Key Point:* It's not enough to know that we need to be on top of our game in each of these areas of our DNA, but also that there is a specific sequence in which to execute them. I believe that a lack of understanding in regard to the sequence of your business's DNA is the biggest reason why 70-80% of contractors are out of business within three years of opening their doors.

You see, when most of us start a business, we are pretty good in a few of these areas of our business' DNA, but if we don't learn the value of the others we are doomed to fail. The sad part is, due to our expertise in these few areas, we can experience initial success and growth. However, without a holistic understanding of your business' DNA, your company is a house of cards just waiting to fall.

As the leaders of our companies, it's our responsibility to be better. If not, we will inevitably let down those we truly care about.

Think about it...

You started your business for a variety of reasons:
- You didn't like the way you were treated at your previous job.
- You didn't like how customers were treated by your previous employer.
- You are a master of quality, and customers want you to provide that quality in your service.
- You are awesome at sales and finally got fed up with using your skills to make someone else rich.

The list goes on and on, but if you really think about it, you started your business because you were good at just a few of the 12 components of a Contractor's DNA. Since then, you've been learning on the fly and wearing a bunch of hats that aren't necessarily your area of expertise. Even worse, you employed your strategies out of order, which is causing you to take one step forward and two steps back.

How do I know this, you ask? I made the same mistake growing my contracting business while using the learn-through-failure approach, and a vast majority of the contractors that come to us want us to help them hire more people so they can grow and scale. The problem is that recruiting, hiring, and onboarding is step #12 in the process. Without the other 11 components of a Contractor's DNA done in sequence, hiring a bunch of people into a broken or partial system is destined for failure.

Once again, I'll ask you to think about it...

If you plan to recruit and hire, you must also systematically train your team. How else will you get them up to speed quickly, so they can start making money and not cost you and your team a tremendous amount of time? If you *can* train them, how will you *produce* everything they're about to sell? If you *can* produce it perfectly, how exactly are you going to *sell* a service that is unique compared to your competitors? If you *do* have a proven repeatable sales system that closes at a higher rate than your competitors, how will you *market* to generate an endless stream of leads for all those new recruits? If you can generate all those leads, sales, and jobs, how will you use *technology* to improve those areas as well as maximize communication and future opportunity from all that data?

That's just the Operational Backbone side of the business! (We will cover those in the second book.)

If you can do all that, how will you hold everyone *accountable* to all the activity and expectations of your system? What will your standards be? How will they get paid in a way that incentivizes them correctly and ensures those expectations are being met and people are held accountable? If you can hold everyone accountable, how will you master your *numbers* and *finances* to make great decisions based on budgets—not your gut—that will keep your organization effective and growing? If you're a financial wizard, how will you *organize* your business to fit the people you're going to hire, culturally, structurally, and legally? If you've got that organization and HR figured out, what *process* will they follow? Are they written down in a way that anyone could follow them without verbal, hand-holding instruction? If you happen to have all those processes defined and written, how will you develop a *culture* driven by your dream and the company's vision that makes everyone want to work for you? Why are you doing what you're doing? Does that inspire others to be a part of it? Last but not least—and really most important—if you've got a killer culture, are you capable? Do you have the *leadership* skills, habits, and capacity to make an epic impact with your business? Without great leadership, all the rest of these strategies mean nothing.

We're going to answer all these questions and give you the strategies and tactics to build that strong foundation your business so desperately needs. By the time you finish this book, you should see the areas where your internal Foundational Backbone is out of sync, and you'll have the strategies and tactics to do something about it. In my next book, you will build off that solid foundation for your business. You will develop everything you need strategically and tactically for all the external Operational Backbone of your business.

Figure 1

Figure 1 will help you visualize the sequence in which the strategies need to be addressed in your business to set a strong foundation.

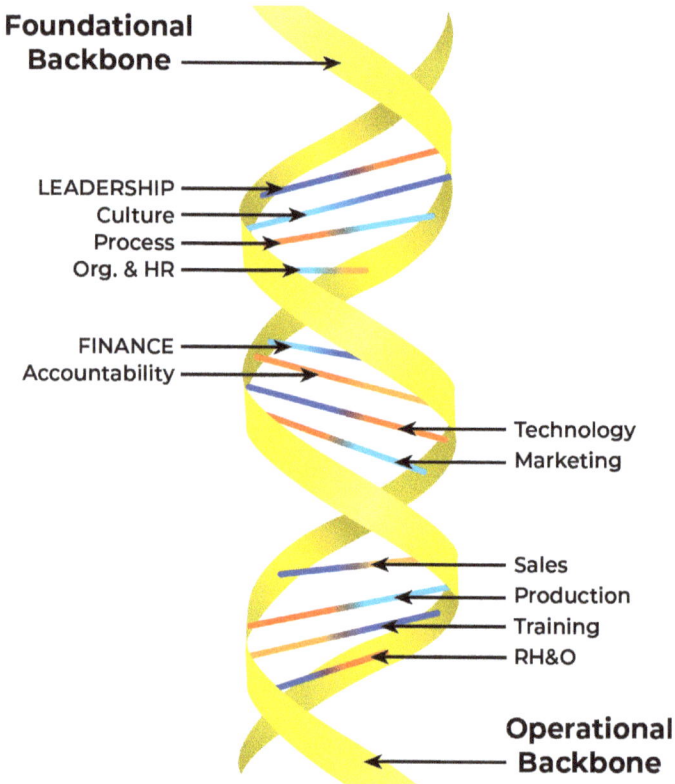

Figure 2

Figure 2 will help you visualize the components of the Contractor DNA and how they impact each other as you continue to grow your business once the foundation is in place.

The Contractor's Blueprint is written in the order in which each component of your DNA should be established. Once you've done so, you will find working on your business instead of in it, will happen naturally because you will easily be able to know what is not working and most importantly, why.

So let's get to it!

Foundational Blueprint Strategy

Chapter 1: Leadership

*Leadership is the ability to motivate
a group of people to act toward
achieving a common goal.*

Belief

It is not enough to simply decide to do something and then take action in an effort to achieve a goal. You have to *absolutely* believe in the worthiness of the pursuit of that goal and the value in achieving it. You have to *absolutely* believe that you have the skill, capacity, and ability to develop a strategy to achieve your goal. Finally, you *absolutely* believe that you will be willing to execute the necessary tactics to make those strategies successful.

I have a feeling that if you went back in time and asked every great leader if they believed in their strategies, they would say "yes." I think if you asked every poor leader, at least when they started, they would say the same. *Key Point:* The difference between success and failure of that belief is a matter of conviction, discipline, and faith. I like to call it "absolute belief." The great leader had conviction in their beliefs, discipline to take the necessary actions, and faith to persevere—he *absolutely believed*. The poor leader did not. The great leader's belief was aligned with who they were and why they were pursuing that belief. The poor leader, on the other hand, was missing this alignment with who they were and why they were pursuing their belief. I find this "identity gap" often in the contractors I coach and most people I engage with. ***Key Point:*** The larger the gap between our "who" and our "why," the less drive we will have to persevere when things get tough. This gap is identified as the difference between our values and our purpose. It is a battle between our internal fulfillment and external expectations. Internally we want to be a particular way but externally we are influenced to do otherwise. When two forces push in opposite directions it causes friction. While some friction can be healthy, too much friction will be too painful to bear.

Whether it is a relationship, spiritual growth, health and wellness, or business, nothing succeeds without belief. Belief in a spouse or new relationship. Belief in a higher power or greater understanding. Belief in exercise and diet as a lifestyle. Belief that you have the ability to start, grow, and ultimately find success in your business as an entrepreneur. The level of conviction, discipline, and faith in that belief will ultimately determine the outcome of each.

All endeavors—great and small, successful or a complete failure—start with incentive. In simplified form, the "it's worth a try" attitude, is the beginning of belief. The amount of belief in whether or not the incentive is *worth the effort* is where conviction comes in. Everything we do starts with incentive, but if we decide to pursue it, it is conviction in that belief that it will pay off in the end.

Here is a simple example: we all brush our teeth (at least I hope we do) because we believe with conviction that if we do, they won't fall out before their time. We do so for the most part twice a day because of discipline. The more often we brush, the stronger our conviction is to our belief, which is based on the incentive. To maintain conviction in our beliefs, we need proof of the incentive. If other people's teeth are staying in longer, then I have proof that brushing works. The beauty of business is that it is easy to see the success of others, making our conviction stronger. It is the discipline to do what is necessary that will determine the outcome of that belief.

JFK spearheaded sending man to the moon. Edison lit the world. Jobs and Gates changed how we perceive technology. I married an amazing woman. Pappy is in heaven…

None of the above would have happened without ultimate conviction, faith in that belief, and the discipline to stick to it.

True, absolute belief makes even the impossible possible. If you don't absolutely believe in your business, have faith you will persevere, or carry the discipline to take the necessary actions to achieve your dreams and goals because of your conviction, stop reading this book and go close your business today. You will fail. All you're doing is creating a business that won't fulfill who you are, which isn't aligned with why you are in business in the first place. I doubt that's why you started your business.

On the other hand, if you absolutely believe and you are willing to learn, you WILL develop a winning strategy, you WILL take Massive Action, you WILL be Disciplined, you WILL persevere, and you WILL make an epic impact because your INCENTIVE will be strong enough to achieve your dreams. The *Contractor's Blueprint* is designed to provide the roadmap—if you have the absolute belief. I hope to empower you to absolutely believe that you can achieve your dreams as you read this book.

You hear a lot these days about taking action, or "massive action." Without absolute belief, you will only take half-hearted action that is full of doubt. Doubt is the enemy of belief. There are a lot of "guru's" out there preaching that in order for you to succeed you simply have to "take action." Action, without absolute belief in your strategy and the tactics of that strategy, is destined to let doubt creep in. We all have doubts, it is part of the human condition, and I find that my level of belief has everything to do with overcoming that doubt or letting it set in. If doubt sets in, you will likely fail. If you don't have absolute belief, you will likely fail. If you fail, you have not only failed yourself, but all of those who trusted you, that you are responsible for, and that BELIEVED in you. Why in the world would you take "massive action" without developing and absolutely believing in your strategy first? It would be like going to war without a plan. I am pretty sure we would have a lot of doubts if we did, and we are likely going to lose. This book is about helping you believe in your ability to win! This doesn't mean that you need to sit down and write a full out 100-page business plan with every last detail, but it does mean you better have some idea of WHERE you are going (dream or goal), HOW you will get there (strategy & tactics), and WHY you're doing it (purpose), that you absolutely believe in.

You see, my superpower is not only 100% absolute belief in myself and my ability to achieve anything I set my mind to if I am disciplined to that belief, but I can also get others to believe in it with me. We are going to achieve each other's goals together. I want to help you to do the same with this book. Maybe—just maybe—if I can give you the plan with the *Contractors Blueprint*, then you will be confident enough to find that unwavering, absolute belief that has been lacking and holding you back from that strategy that is necessary to take the massive action required to make an epic impact.

When you can get others to believe in your vision and make them believe that they will benefit from helping you reach that vision, you achieve "buy-in." As long as you follow through on those promises, you will become a leader. How great of a leader? Well, that depends.

Before we talk about following through and being a great leader, we need to understand exactly what we are leading.

I don't think most people were sitting in high school thinking about owning or working for a contracting business. Most of us had big dreams of being doctors, musicians, astronauts, athletes, or something else we could be "proud" to say we do when asked. Well, here we sit; we ended up as contractors...

The truth is, we're so much more than "just" a contractor! We build things, we make things beautiful, we keep families safe. We also lead teams, provide tons of jobs, solve big problems, understand finance, provide for our families, and become experts that allow us to sell our services.

Best of all, if we do it right, we can change the lives of our customers, teammates, community, nation, and maybe even the world, but only if you absolutely believe you can.

In other words, our contracting business is the vehicle we have chosen to achieve our dreams, and it can be the vehicle for others to do likewise! Now that's something to be proud of!

This book is designed to help you gain that belief by providing you with a strategic and tactical blueprint that will allow you to scale your business to any size and allow you to make that epic impact you may not even know you are capable of yet. In order to make an epic impact the first thing we need to do is create the capacity to accomplish more in less time.

Let's get to work on creating the capacity you will need to be a great leader!

The most important thing I've learned about leadership is how to create *capacity*. There are only 24 hours in a day, and there's no way you can do everything it will take to make your company great in the time allotted to you—without help. You need help from others, mentors, technology, and automation. It is all about creating the capacity to achieve more in less time. Leadership is all about creating capacity to work on your business, not in it. This chapter is all about increasing your capacity to do so. I created an equation to help you remember the importance of this.

(Ability) x (Capacity) = Impact?

Key Point: Your ability as a leader multiplied by your capacity as a leader equals the amount of impact you will have exponentially. In other words, the more skilled you become as a leader, the more you are able to grow other leaders in your company. This affords you more time to work on your business instead of in it and increases the impact you will have on a grand scale. It's actually pretty simple. Know what you're great at and find others to lead what you suck at, thus giving you more time to focus on your strengths. Our biggest enemies to success are selfishness, greed, and pride. All lead to the ridiculous belief that we have to do it all, because no one else is capable of doing what we can do.

In order to become a great leader, you have to learn what type of leader you are. By identifying your strengths, you can delegate your weaknesses to others. Next, you have to understand that your personality as a leader will play a huge role in your leadership strategy. Finally, you have to be totally dedicated to the skill and habits of a great leader and continually improve on them.

Let's develop your leadership strategy...

Leadership Types

Which one are you?

Disclaimer: If you've done any reading on leadership, you'll have read all kinds of information on the various types of leaders. There have been a billion books written on leadership. A lot of those are really good, and there are even a few great ones. Some of the content in this chapter can be found in any number of these books. The rest of the content is unique to what I have learned. What makes this book different is how it all fits together. There's an order to things, and the first strategy in that order that you need to absolutely nail is your Leadership Strategy. Without getting this strategy right, all the rest will be meaningless.

To keep it simple, there are three types of leaders[1]. There are Idealists, Realists, and Champions. The key is figuring out which one you *really* are, being good with that, realizing the importance of each type to the overall success of your business, and understanding how they relate to each other.

I will caution you here not to get caught up in a fantasy of who you think you are as a leader. When I ask, "what kind

---

1   This has been written about dozens of times as Idealist, Integrator, Specialist or Dreamer, Implementer, Specialist and a host of other variations. I chose the words I did because of their core meaning and how they apply overall to the needed leaders in a business. Credit needs to be given to Gino Wickman, the author of Traction, for the relationship between Idealist and Implementer, and in the case of this book, Realist, where we will further define the role of this type of leader.

of leader do you think you are?" most people respond with, "Idealist." Now, a lot of entrepreneurs are Idealists—don't get me wrong—but don't get caught up with the perceived importance of being an Idealist. If you really are, your skills won't be needed for long.

Idealists

Idealists tend to be visionaries and dreamers. They are uber creative, and they can "see" in their mind's eye the future of the business and how successful it will be. They are also the driver of the business and normally extroverts. They are sometimes described as ADD. They tend to lack when it comes to focusing on the details of tasks but never lose sight of the overall goal. They despise being held accountable, but they are the ones that drive endless opportunity for the business. Their passion is palpable, and you want to be on their team.

Realists

Realists, on the other hand, are driven by process and are amazing problem solvers. They "hear" the Idealist and are able to distill their ideas down to the most valuable and likely way to succeed. Realists are excellent at identifying the best way to implement a new idea or how to solve a problem with an initiative that's going sideways. They are sometimes described as OCD, usually characterized as an introvert, and are normally driven by metrics, data, and results. The Realist is your accountability expert.

Champions

Champions are the most overlooked but are absolutely key to scaling a business. They are technical experts in very specific areas. They have a "particular set of skills" [insert Liam Neesom voice here], and they are chomping at the bit to use them—if you would just ask, because they will rarely ask you. They tend to be perfectionists and are sometimes plagued by "paralysis by analysis." Champions are oftentimes described as introverts unless it relates to their area of expertise. They are more than willing to add to the discussion when they perceive they have a strength on that topic. They ask a ton of questions to ensure they don't make any mistakes. Once given authority they will take ownership and want to be held accountable. They will absolutely fight for the area they lead and are extremely loyal.

Now that we have the three types, I want to be clear about something. It is extremely rare to have someone that is just one type, and there will always be a little overlap. However, you will likely find that you are stronger in one area than the others. It is even more rare to have an individual who is strong in two or possibly even three. These are generational leaders, and you'll know them when you see them.

Idealists need Realists to keep them in check and get them to focus on the most important initiatives now while being smart enough to give them time to create. Realists need Idealists to keep coming up with those big ideas so they can see the whole picture, help determine what to do now and then solve the problem of getting it done. Both Idealists and Realists need Champions to execute on those initiatives. Champions need Idealists and Realists to give them purpose and possibly the mentorship to become an Idealist, or more likely a Realist themselves.

The largest companies in the world understand the dynamic between the leadership types and have learned how to use it to their advantage. We can do the same.

Some quick examples...

Microsoft
Bill Gates is the Idealist that is also skilled in being a Realist—and even a Champion when it comes to writing code. Without Paul Allen, a Realist who had the ability to sift through Bill's ideas and identify what works, there is no Microsoft as we see it today. Paul Allen was also a Champion when it comes to code writing.

Apple
Steve Jobs was the Idealist. Steve Wozniak is a Realist. He took Job's ideas and sifted through them to identify the right ingredients and made them reality. Without Steve Wozniak, Apple likely wouldn't exist.

Google
Larry Page is an Idealist Extraordinaire, but without Sergey Brin the Realist—you guessed it—you're still searching on Yahoo.

As you can see, the team of an Idealist and Realist can accomplish great things in the beginning, but without recognizing the value of Champions, they would not be what they are today.

Bill Gates could see the value of Microsoft Office and had the ability to write the code. If he had done that, he wouldn't have had the time to work on a thousand other ideas. Paul Allen took that idea and worked out the details and processes, but it wouldn't be what it is today without a Word Champion, an Excel Champion, a Publisher Champion and several other Champions that make Microsoft Office what it is today.

The same could be said of Apple, Google, Disney, and the list goes on extolling the virtues of the Idealist, Realist, and Champion dynamic.

The key is to figure out which one you are. If you say you're an Idealist but you're not creative or forward thinking, you're probably not an Idealist. If you have a lot of turnover and have a hard time getting people to work for you, you're probably not an Idealist. If you constantly get focused on the details and lose sight of the big picture, you're probably not an Idealist.

If you're constantly dreaming up new ideas and getting them halfway done, you're probably not a Realist. If you're always letting everyone know how great your company is going to be you're probably not a Realist. If everyone wants to work for you, you're probably not a Realist.

The cool thing is that you're probably a Champion! Remember those two or three reasons you started your business? You're likely a Champion in those. You're the Sales Champion, the Quality Champion, and the Recruiting Champion. While that is awesome and something to be proud of, and your business wouldn't exist otherwise, you will need to find other Champions in your area of expertise to reach your full capacity as the Idealist or Realist your business needs.

What type of leader are you?

Are you an Idealist or Realist?

What are some of your options for finding your Leadership alter ego of Idealist or Realist?
- Identify and grow the leader you need?
- Recruit a known leader in the area you need help?
- Bring on a partner to balance you out?

What areas are you a Champion in?

What areas will you need to find new Champion leaders for?

Leadership Personality

Now that we have the leadership types down, let's talk about leadership personalities.

While the skill and habits of leaders are largely the same and can be learned by anyone, leadership personalities vary greatly. We'll cover the skill and habits in the next part of this chapter.

When it comes to leadership personality, you need to keep the definition of a leader in mind. A leader is one who has the ability to lead others in pursuit of a common goal or purpose. That's it—no more, no less. You'll notice it doesn't say a "good" leader. In my opinion, there is no such thing as a "good" leader, or a "bad" one for that matter. Leadership can be "great" or "poor," but not "good" or "bad," because what one perceives as "good," could be "bad" to another. Leadership is not a talent or a title, *it is a way of being.*

For example, Mother Teresa is oftentimes described as a good person who was a great leader, but there were many non-Christian people who thought she was bad. Very few of those people wouldn't say she wasn't a great leader though. The results were obvious.

I'm sure we can all think of various leaders we would personally describe as good or bad, but in reality, they were all "great" leaders or we wouldn't even know their names. Why? Because they had an extraordinary ability to motivate many in pursuit of a common purpose, and they knew how to create capacity to do more by growing other leaders. As a result, they made enough of an impact to be remembered. The really interesting thing is that the ones who put others first, like Mother Theresa, have a legacy that continues on and grows. The ones who put their own ambitions first have a legacy that slowly dies and is only held onto by a few radical zealots. The latter is a great example of a misalignment between one's who and why, where internal character is at odds with external purpose.

In business, there are four personalities of leaders: Democratic, Autocratic, Hero, and Villain. Very rarely is anyone all one personality. They will normally have a dominant personality and a subordinate personality. Before we jump to conclusions on what personality of a leader we are, let's get a better understanding of the four personalities.

The first two personalities have to do with the nature of an individual and how they interact with people. In other words, they are intrinsically wired this way due to past experiences and their social environment. These personalities are normally developed from early childhood through their first successes in the working world. This environment has shaped how they perceive what works as a leader to be successful.

Democratic
A Democratic leader is more likely to want consensus from the team on decisions. They want to make sure everyone is onboard in the pursuit of a new initiative. They will have their own strong opinion on what the decision should be, but they will listen to reason when outnumbered by the team's well thought out reasoning. The will of the people matters to them.

Autocratic
An Autocratic leader is more likely to drive their decisions and path based on their own experiences and what they think is best for the future of their team. Although they will listen to others input, the final decision is always theirs. They are driven by metrics, results, and goals— even at the expense of a teammate. In other words, it's their way or the highway.

The next two personality types have to do with "motive." In other words, why do they lead the way they do? The factors that determine motive are extrinsic, or outside circumstances. The way these outside circumstances are perceived by the individual will justify their reasoning.

Hero
The Hero leader is more likely to make sacrifices personally to serve the greater good of the people. They genuinely care about people and empathize with them. They tend to be driven by a moral compass and focus on recognizing and encouraging others. Righteousness and justice rule their decision making.

Villain
The Villain leader is driven by personal achievement. They tend to be described as stubborn because they are less likely to agree with others. They are extremely task oriented and money motivated, although the money is usually a byproduct of a need to prove all the naysayers wrong. In their mind, the end justifies the means, and results drive their decisions.

Before we go any further, I want to address the Villain leadership personality. We thought long and hard about that name, and much credit is due here to Nathan Tebedo, our Lead Coach at Contractor Coach PRO. He deserves credit not just for the naming convention of Villain but for this whole section on Leadership Personalities. He actually inspired this part of the book when he approached me about a conversation on leadership styles and whether there are good or evil leaders. Nathan is a natural philosopher, and these are the types of things that rattle around in his brain all the time. You are benefiting today from a conversation and thought initiated by Nathan, and he deserves a ton of credit for helping us both think it through on several occasions. It is invaluable in our coaching to understand who we're working with and invaluable to our clients to give them insight, not only into themselves but into all their leaders and potential leaders.

As far as the word "villain" goes, it's not necessarily a bad thing. Remember Mother Teresa? Well, she was a villain to those that didn't believe in what she believed in. We heavily considered using "victim" or "victor" instead, but the reality is that a villain can be a great leader while a victim never will. C'mon all you sports and comic book fans—how many times have you rooted for the villain!? Why? Because you can relate! You can see yourself in their position, and you align with what they are after, which just might be the right thing.

In order to determine our leadership personality, we need to ask ourselves two questions:
1. Are we goal driven or people driven?
2. Are we driven by motive or nature?

The answers to these two questions are paramount in understanding your own leadership personality.

Let's dig into those two questions now that you have a better understanding of the personalities and why they are named the way they are. The big thing is to not get hung up on the personality name. This is for your own education. It's not like you're going to run around saying, "I'm a Villain Leader!" Although, there may be a few of you out there that would relish the role of playing the Villain. I know I did at one point.

Look at Figure 1.1 on the next page. I think from the descriptions, it's pretty easy for you to identify which personality is your dominant one. The subordinate personality is the one you keep thinking, "I'm a lot like that too though."

MOTIVE

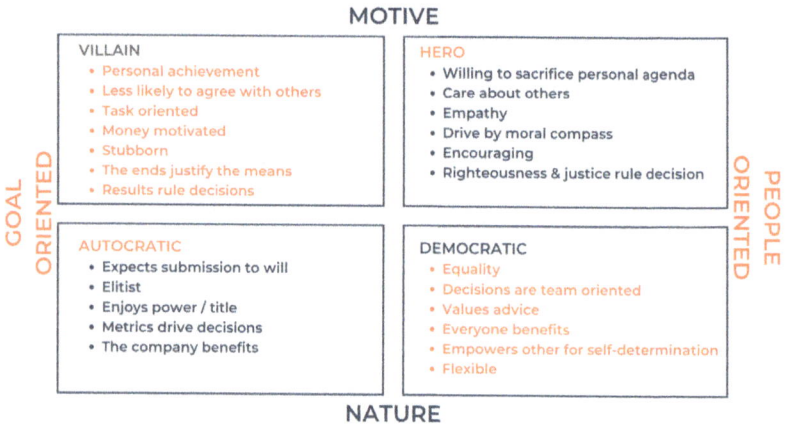

VILLAIN
- Personal achievement
- Less likely to agree with others
- Task oriented
- Money motivated
- Stubborn
- The ends justify the means
- Results rule decisions

HERO
- Willing to sacrifice personal agenda
- Care about others
- Empathy
- Drive by moral compass
- Encouraging
- Righteousness & justice rule decision

AUTOCRATIC
- Expects submission to will
- Elitist
- Enjoys power / title
- Metrics drive decisions
- The company benefits

DEMOCRATIC
- Equality
- Decisions are team oriented
- Values advice
- Everyone benefits
- Empowers other for self-determination
- Flexible

GOAL ORIENTED

PEOPLE ORIENTED

NATURE

Figure 1.1

For many of you, your first instinct will be to gravitate toward Hero. Who doesn't want to be a hero?

But...

If you're driven by results and goals over people, the truth of the matter is that you're more likely to be perceived as a Villain. Others will gravitate toward Democratic, but again, if the goal outweighs the people, you're more likely to be an Autocratic leader. The key is to be honest with yourself because there's a bit of good news here. If you don't like the Leadership Personality you are, you can change it! It's hard work, and you'll have to be constantly vigilant to your motive, nature, goals, and people, but if you want to be a Hero/Democratic leader, you can. It will be easier to change your motive than your nature though. Motives are determined by external circumstances. When those circumstances change, a Villain can become a Hero and a Hero a Villain, literally overnight. It happens all the time in comic books, and if you're observant then you've seen it in the real world too. Your nature is internal though and much harder to change. It takes discipline and constant dedication to shift your nature, but even then, when it comes down to crisis, you are likely to revert to your original natural self. Remember this is a book on strategy; all of the leadership personalities have proven successful to varying degrees. It's truly up to you on what approach to take with your specific strategy. If I would have known about these personalities earlier in my entrepreneurial journey, I would have probably made some different decisions along the way. I hope to help you not make those same mistakes.

My early Leadership Personality was the product of being raised as a step son who was constantly told I wouldn't amount to anything and my first work experiences that expected long hours with little reward and high pressure. You see many young leaders are driven by similar situations and their external environments. Everyone is telling them they can't do something or change themselves in some way and believing this is what the world expects of them. Many will strive at all costs to do what others say they can't and to obtain signs of success, all to prove to others that they are successful so they can earn the approval they believe they need.

I know because I was a Villain/Autocratic leader.

When I was younger, I didn't really care a whole lot about whether anyone liked me, what they were dealing with personally, or anything else other than "winning." Employees and colleagues were simply game pieces on a chessboard to me, and I was playing to win. Everything was a competition to me, and my attitude was to win at all costs. We've all heard the saying, "if you ain't cheatin', you're not tryin'!" Let's just say I was trying really hard, and at first, I achieved everything I set out to do. I built a $25 million dollar business in less than three years, on three separate occasions! I had fancy cars and trucks, a huge house, boats, ATV's, and all the toys. Whatever

I wanted to do, I did. And whatever I wanted to buy, I bought. I had proven all the naysayers wrong, and I had done it my way. I could, and I did!

If that's what you're after, more power to you. But if you look back at that story, you'll see I said the words, "I," "me," or "my" 15 times. When it's all about you, you will always be striving to *get more*. The only problem is that there is only so much to *get*, but we *think* we never have enough to *prove* ourselves to others. I'm not here to lecture you, and I'm sure you've heard a lot of this before. But believe me when I say, "when it changes from 'getting' to 'giving' and your 'who' is aligned with your 'why,' your whole life will change to feeling fulfilled." You'll quit feeling like there's never enough, and you'll start feeling like YOU are enough! There's no better feeling in all the world than knowing that you are enough. ***Key Point:*** When you realize that life isn't just about you, you will stop seeking the approval of others, and you will approve of yourself. When you approve of yourself, you gain freedom from the unrealistic expectations that the outside world has set for you. You gain the freedom to be what God intended you to be.

It all changed for me the day I was sitting on the front step of my huge house. Everything was crumbling down around me. A bookkeeper who was also a partner in our business had embezzled $500k+ from our business. My other partner, my best friend, just couldn't get past it, wanted out, and wanted to prosecute our bookkeeper at all costs. To top it all off, the bookkeeper and her husband went out on their own and stole something even more valuable, our people, to start their own contracting business. It went so far as my top salesperson, a friend I had recruited like crazy because I knew he'd be great. I still think about it to this day. Was he a chess piece or was he a friend—someone I cared about? He and his wife joined forces with them, even after we had shown them the bookkeeper's transgressions in black and white. The opportunity to own a company outweighed the risk.

Remember, I'm sitting on the front step of my huge house, looking at all my things. While I had achieved all my goals and had the money I needed, none of it brought me joy. None of it *proved* anything. I had lost my best friend and partner. I couldn't understand why our bookkeeper would stab us in the back when she was in a better position than she had ever been before. My top sales rep was gone. Half our team went with him. My business—my empire—was doomed without them. What would my family think? Would my wife lose faith in me and want a divorce? Would my kids think less of me? What would all the naysayers have to say?

Like many of us do when we feel like hope is lost, I began to pray. I prayed like I never had before. It was raw and emotional. At first, it was a selfish prayer. "God, help me save my company… God, help me find a way to pay our bills." Then it turned into a prayer of smite! "God, please rain havoc on that good-for-nothing bookkeeper! God, teach those ungrateful sales reps a lesson so they understand that I made them!" (Again, a bunch of "I's" and "me's." Being stubborn is such a villain thing to be.) Then my prayers began to change. It started with forgiveness. "God, forgive me for all the sins I've waged for my business… God, forgive me for not trusting you in my business and life… God, forgive me for not being a better person." Next came submission and tears. "God, I trust you and what you have in store for me… God, it is not about me, but it's all about you… God, please tell me what to do, and I will do it without question—I promise."

The answer to that last prayer changed my life and my leadership personality forever. My motives changed right then and there.

I've heard people say, "God spoke to me and told me to do such and such." I expected that to be a loud, booming voice from Heaven with clear instructions. Maybe for others it is. But for me, it was more of a feeling, just like when I resigned later in life with a single word repeating over and over again inside my head...

"Serve, serve, serve."

I took that as the only answer I was going to get, and I've done my best to do so every day since. I'm pretty sure God doesn't like broken promises. I have backslid, of course. I'm human, and humans are imperfect. But now that I'm mindful of it, I get back on track because it's not about "I," it's about "you." And it's not about "me," It's about God working through me for "we."

Here's the craziest thing of all. The more I serve and give out of genuine love for another without an expected return, the more I receive, allowing me to serve and give more. This book is a culmination of my need to serve and give more.

Now, whether you're a God person or not, people are more likely to help those that help them, rather than those who help themselves. It's hard to be mean to someone who loves you and puts you first.

All of these leadership personalities can achieve great success. Some fleeting, some a legacy.

Which Leadership Personality do you have?

Do you feel drawn to become another?

Leadership Skills & Habits

A lot of people believe that leadership is some kind of blessing received at birth, like a God given talent. Nothing could be further from the truth. Leadership comes down to skills and habits anyone can learn. Having the discipline to exercise that skill and live those habits is the difference between a great leader and a poor one.

Once again, there have been a ton of books extolling the virtues of the exact set of skills that make a great leader. I've read most of them, but the more I read the more difficult it seems to keep up with them all. There have got to be somewhere around 35 different skills that I've read and learned about that you "absolutely must have" to be a great leader. The reality is that the world is telling us what to be again, and there's no way anyone can be great at all of them! It can leave your head spinning.

After coaching more than 400 clients, having another 1,500+ on our learning platform, and speaking to over 50,000 through various speaking engagements, it has become painfully clear that it's really all about what I call a "Super Skill" that has 7 Leadership Habits. When you learn these 7 Leadership Habits and make them part of who you are as a leader, you're destined to be a great and well-respected leader.

First, let's start with the Super Skill: *Connection*. If you become a great communicator who truly connects with others, you can become a great leader. To be clear, connecting through communication isn't just the ability to transmit verbal instruction. That's only a part of it. Great communicators who learn how to connect and understand the power of words, both spoken and written (the single most destructive and constructive tool known to the human race), also understand the power of listening, questions, body language, their actions, their behaviors, and their love. They understand the power of connection. *Key Point:* Connection is knowing what someone needs and when they need it all while being willing to give it. You probably know someone like this. When they enter the room, they are revered and respected, but they are also completely accessible and approachable. You don't want to miss a word they say. They know how to connect.

If you think about it, leaders fail by not listening, not asking questions, not getting things in writing, saying one thing but doing another, not bringing the energy, not showing what to do but still expecting nothing less than perfection, and, probably most of all, not caring more about others. All of which are forms of connecting through communication to develop the one thing no one can take away from you: your reputation. In other words, you are either a person of your word or not. These words are not just reflected verbally or in writing. You're "saying something" each time you make an expression, move your body, listen to understand, take an action, and even with each decision you make. You are either connecting or disconnecting with those you are looking to lead. When you disconnect with people, they lose faith in you, your vision, and how it applies to their goals. They go from believing they have a career with purpose to a job without meaning or recognition. They go from believing they are a *part* of something to believing they are a *piece* of something. They have already left, and you don't even know it yet.

So, what are the 7 Leadership Habits that create connection? Well, like you'll see throughout this book, there is a running theme. There's an order to things. By doing these 7 Leadership Habits in order and repeating them over and over, we connect and gain what we need as leaders: belief. We gain that belief through our Super Skill to connect by using our Leadership Habits. First, let's list them in order, then discuss how each communicates your leadership and connects you with others.

1. Engage
2. Educate
3. Example
4. Empathy
5. Encourage
6. Empower
7. Expect

Before we discuss each and their value to your leadership, I want you to understand this is by no means an exhaustive list of skills and habits for leaders. As I mentioned before, any number of authors on leadership have all kinds of skills you can choose from. These are simply the 7 Leadership Habits that will have the most impact on your leadership. There are other skills and habits you may want to learn over time, but for our purposes in the *Contractor's Blueprint*, these are the 7 Leadership Habits you *must* develop to get buy-in, activity, discipline, results, and belief in order to truly connect with your team. A connected team is a cohesive unit all working toward a common goal. A chain that cannot be broken!

First, we have to ***Engage***. Engaging others in our vision (which will be discussed further in the chapter on Culture), reminding our team often of that vision, and letting them know that they play a crucial role in making that vision a reality determines our success as a leader. This vision is not just about the business and their role in that business, but how it relates to achieving our goals and how we will personally invest in them and their families as human beings to achieve their individual goals. I've often invited the spouse of a potential teammate to an interview to get them engaged as well. Until someone understands what is in it for them, it's hard to gain buy-in.

Next, we have to **Educate**. Not just our new recruits, but all of our teammates and ourselves as well. We have to communicate an understanding that we are here to get better every day. Through education and experience comes confidence, through confidence comes competence, and through competence comes creativity. When people become creative, they become innovative, staying one step ahead of the competition. (We'll cover more on this in the chapter on Training in my next book.) Educating your team solidifies *buy-in* and starts to generate *activity*.

Following closely on the heels of education comes the **Example** habit. We have to set an example every day. We don't ask anyone to do something that we can't show them how to do and be willing to do ourselves. We never compromise our Core Values (more on this in the chapter on Culture). We don't bring drama into the building. If we do, it sends a message that it's okay for everyone else to do the same. If we aren't satisfied with the team around us and find ourselves complaining about that team, the first thing we have to do is look at ourselves in the mirror and ask, "who am I attracting and what am I modeling for them?" Your team will become what you are, so be what you want your team to be! Your example solidifies *activity* and starts to inspire *discipline*.

Next is **Empathy**, the second most dangerous habit when misunderstood. Empathy is the ability to understand and share the feelings of another. In other words, caring. Be careful here though. Care too much and you will enable and entitle others to take advantage of you and your team. Care not enough and you'll lose them to someone who does. You can't lose sight of the fact that you have experience that they don't. You have to get really good at remembering what it was like when you were learning and put yourself in their shoes. You also need to keep in mind that they may be experiencing something personally that you aren't and that you possibly never have. Get to know your team, and when something just doesn't seem right, connect with questions and try to be understanding of their situation in an effort to come to a solution together. Your empathy underscores the importance of their *discipline* and the likely results of that discipline.

Next, we have **Encouragement**. We must recognize effort and hard work even when the end result might be failure. Unfortunately, it seems we're hard wired as humans to focus on the negative. It's why someone can do something right ten times in a row and hear nothing, but boy, is there hell to pay on that eleventh time when they screw up. I really find the "shit sandwich" approach most successful here when someone screws up. First, I start with something good they did (a slice of tasty bread), then we discuss the failing (the shit), and I finish with how much I believe in them and their ability (another slice of tasty bread). Our ability to look for what someone has done well, recognize it, and encourage more of it solidifies *discipline* and starts getting *results*.

Empowerment is my favorite of the 7 Leadership Habits. It's a sign that someone's *buy-in, activity, discipline,* and *results* deserve opportunity. Empowerment is the beginning of growing new leaders who will, at some point, give us more capacity by freeing up our time to work on our business rather than in it! This is where most poor leaders screw up. God knows I have! You can ruin a potentially great leader by giving them too much authority too quickly. The best example I can think of is taking a great salesperson and making them a sales manager without any training or empowerment in smaller areas of responsibility first. Yeah, I know—you've never empowered someone by giving them a title and leaving them to figure it out. Me neither [insert knowing wink here]. Instead, when you identify a potential leader, start giving them small opportunities like running a training for the team on something they do well, or assigning them a project they are passionate about that will be a part of the duties of the title you want to give them in the future. Empowerment will solidify their *results* and start to justify their *belief* in you as a leader.

Finally, we come to **Expect**. The most dangerous of the habits and the hardest for leaders to implement. For as tough as the reputation of a contractor is, we are like the Grinch when it comes to confrontation; our heart grows three sizes that day. If you don't hold people accountable to the expectations that were set and agreed upon, to put it simply, you don't love them, and you're failing them as a leader they can respect. You enable them—much like the dangers of empathy—to take advantage of your kindness. Once you give in, it sends a message that communicates to the whole team that your expectations don't mean anything.

Key Point: To truly know if people are meeting expectations, you have to *Inspect What You Expect*. For numbers and metrics, it's easy if you're tracking them (we'll get more into these in the chapter on Accountability) but for your core values, your processes, and your procedures, you have to watch. Initiatives like "Ride Alongs" and "Day with the Leader" can really open your eyes and theirs. When someone isn't meeting expectations, it must be communicated immediately, a course of action must be agreed upon, coaching must ensue, and an understanding of this situation as a strike against their aspirations with your company must be established. If you look at it for what it is, we are in the position of providing "tough love" (just as we would to a child we love) in order to help them achieve their potential and avoid mistakes.

The most difficult thing I have ever had to do was fire one of our top salespeople. Although I genuinely loved them, I loved my team even more. It wasn't about their numbers—those were awesome! I could count on $1-$1.5 million from them every year. Unfortunately, their monetary success came with a cost. They weren't adhering to our core value of honesty or our purpose "to make it easy." As a matter of fact, they made it harder every day on me, our staff, and our customers. We had met, decided on an agreed course of action, and dealt with a strike two that included a further course of action in the hopes that there wouldn't be a strike three. Unfortunately, even with the warning, course of action, and coaching, there was ultimately a strike three.

When I called them into my office and shared how the course of action hadn't been followed, their exact words were, with a hint of laughter in their voice, "I guess now you have to fire me." The laughter subsided quickly when I said that is exactly what we were going to do and why I had to do it. I told him it was because I loved him so much that I had to let him go. I let him know that his path was one of destruction—not just for him or our team, but for his marriage, his family, and ultimately his reputation. I hoped this would be the event that woke him up. I also explained that I loved the team, which was more important than any one individual, and that if I didn't do this, I would be sending the wrong message to them. I still remember the tears in both of our eyes as he left my office like it was yesterday. It was a defining moment for me as a leader and for them as a person—as it will be for you when, not *if*, you are faced with a similar situation.

Within 5 minutes, my phone started ringing.

Teammate: "Did you really fire [redacted]?"

Me: "Yes, they weren't representing the standards we expect here."

Teammate: "Thank you."

That simple "thank you" was the only confirmation I needed to know that I had done the right thing for the company and, ultimately, the team.

There was a noticeable shift in demeanor right away. Other sales reps picked up their production. Administrative staff were smiling instead of complaining. Our production team wasn't pulling out their hair. The best part was that we beat all of our projections that year. All because I led by *expecting* our standards to be met and being accountable to those standards.

Years later, that rep came back to me and thanked me. They explained that at first they were extremely pissed at me, but after thinking about it over the years they realized that experience had changed the course of their life for the better. Later in the month that I fired them, their spouse served them divorce papers, which was the final wake up call. That day, they vowed to change their ways to salvage their marriage, family, and reputation. Today they own a thriving roofing business. The thing I remember most about that conversation is them telling me how much respect they had for me and what I had to do that day. They said they use that example in their own business. That is what *Expectation* is all about: respect. ***Key Point:*** Respect is earned, not given, and takes a long time to get only to be lost in the blink of an eye when you don't follow through on your word. Remember, your reputation is the one thing you control that no one can take away from you. Expectations solidify *belief* in you as a leader.

These 7 Leadership Habits of the Super Skill of Connection initially happen in a specific order, but they never stop. You must make it a habit to engage others in your vision often, educate every day, set the example all the time, show empathy always, encourage others by recognizing their contributions as they happen, empower those who have earned it to grow a continuous flow of leaders that afford you more capacity to grow yourself and your business, and finally, inspect what you expect and hold people accountable because you genuinely love them and your reputation as a leader is on the line. We describe it as "Leadership Torque" (see Figure 1.2). A great analogy would be to imagine your leadership as the wheel of a car. You are the engine, drivetrain, and axle that drives everything around you. The 7 Leadership Habits are the rim of that wheel that transfers the torque from you to where the rubber meets the road with your team, buy-in, activity, discipline, results, and belief. Just like the amount of torque you apply when you drive your vehicle, you need to press the gas just right to move forward at the right speed without spinning out. This approach creates a healthy tension between you and your team, with just the right amount of pressure to drive together in effort to reach a common goal.

Figure 1.2

So now you should know the type of leader you are, the personality of your leadership style, and the skill and habits it will take to connect with others and lead your business.

What will your Leadership Strategy be?

What tactics will you use to execute your Leadership Strategy?

Here are some ways to improve your leadership:

1. Read, read, and read some more! - there is a Leadership Reading List in the Resources section at the back of this book.
2. Time Management - there's never enough time in the day to handle all the responsibilities we have as leaders. The biggest reason is our inability to manage our time. Stop letting everyone else manage your time for you. This doesn't mean we don't make ourselves available, it just means we let everyone know when we're available. The best solution I've found for this is to create a "Leadership Schedule" and let everyone know it's how you'll be operating from now on to give your best in serving them. This must include your entire day, both personal and business wise. Start with your personal stuff first, or there won't be any time for that once you get done with the business.
   - First, the personal stuff. Block off time for when you wake up, when you eat, when you work out, when you work on yourself, when you spend time with family, when you'll have date night, when you'll read, and when you'll sleep.
   - Next, address the business. When you go on sales calls, when you make follow-up calls, when you follow-up with vendors, when you send emails and texts, when you do payroll, when you have open office hours, when you have meetings, etc. Most importantly include a block of time to work on your business instead of in it.

Whether you have 30 minutes or a couple of hours a week, the time you spend now pays huge dividends in the future. Last but not least, include time to connect with your team by allowing time for your 7 Leadership Habits. This is nothing specific to a person, customer, or duty, just the general time in which your duties will fall (see an example on Figure 1.3). Now is the time to communicate it, explain why you're using it and how it will benefit others, and finally post it.

Time	Monday	Tuesday	Wednesday	Thursday	Friday	Saturday	Sunday
6:00 AM	Wake	Wake	Wake	Wake	Wake	Wake	
6:30 AM	Exercise	Exercise	Exercise	Exercise	Exercise	Exercise	
7:00 AM							
7:30 AM	Team Text and Daily Sales Report	Team Text and Daily Sales Report	Team Text and Daily Sales Report	Team Text and Daily Sales Report	Team Text and Daily Sales Report	Team Text and Daily Sales Report	
8:00 AM	Priorities and Tasks	Priorities and Tasks	Priorities and Tasks	Priorities and Tasks	Priorities and Tasks	Sales Practice	
8:30 AM							
9:00 AM	Sold Jobs update, reviews, and approvals	Sold Jobs update, reviews, and approvals	Sold Jobs update, reviews, and approvals	Sold Jobs update, reviews, and approvals	Sold Jobs update, reviews, and approvals		
9:30 AM							
10:00 AM							
10:30 AM	Emails & Phone Calls	Emails & Phone Calls	Production Meeting	Emails & Phone Calls	Emails & Phone Calls	Field Time w/Team	
11:00 AM							
11:30 AM	Coaching	Coaching		Coaching	Update Level 10 Agenda		
12:00 PM	Lunch	Lunch	Lunch	Lunch	Lunch		
12:30 PM							
1:00 PM	Sales Practice	1-on-1's	1-on-1's	Updt Sales Reports	Level 10 Meeting		Day off
1:30 PM							
2:00 PM		Improve My Game		Improve My Game			
2:30 PM	Update Notes on Jobs		Update Notes on Jobs		Update Notes on Jobs		
3:00 PM							
3:30 PM							
4:00 PM	Emails & Phone Calls	In the Field Inspecting What I Expect, Training and Coaching	Emails & Phone Calls	In the Field Inspecting What I Expect, Training and Coaching	Emails & Phone Calls	Family Time	
4:30 PM							
5:00 PM	Put Out Fires		Put Out Fires				
5:30 PM							
6:00 PM							
6:30 PM							
7:00 PM					Family Time		
7:30 PM							
8:00 PM							
8:30 PM							
9:00 PM							
9:30 PM							
10:00 PM							
10:30 PM							
11:00 PM							

Figure 1.3

You'll find really quickly that you get more done in less time because people aren't just barging into your office, you're not answering every call, email, or text like it's life and death, you're not reacting, and you're being proactive. People will start to be less reliant on you to be the contracting encyclopedia, and they will start to solve their own problems, allowing you even more time to work on it, not in it.

3. Set a recurring weekly mission meeting with your management team. (If you don't have a management team yet, this is the time in your schedule to work on your business).
   • Your weekly mission meeting should be focused on the challenges your team is facing, the tasks that need to be done by who and when, reporting on your current progress toward your yearly mission (more on this in the chapter on Culture), and what adjustments might need to be made.
   • You're always focused on the most important thing you can do right now to achieve your mission.
   • If you're really trying to get the most out of your meetings, we suggest sitting down with one of our coaches to launch our advanced mission meeting with your team. You'll be amazed at what your team can accomplish with a mission meeting.[2]
4. Start identifying which leader you need to balance your own leadership style (Idealist or Realist) and start empowering them with small projects to grow them into that leadership role. Do likewise with your Champions.
5. Last but not least, don't forget about you. Take care of your spiritual self, your health, and your mind. The longer you're around and sharp, the more likely you are to leave a lasting legacy. Sharpen that axe so you can work smarter not harder.

---

2   If you would like a copy of our simplified mission meeting, go to https://bit.ly/CCPMAP

"There's only one you, make the most of it."
—Bud Wallace (a.k.a. Pappy)

"Do as much as you can for whoever you can, for as long as you can."
—Adolph Johnson

I'll end this chapter with some guidance from the greatest leader to ever walk this earth on what it means to truly lead. He must have known what he was talking about since he has more than 2.3 billion followers and continues to grow daily almost 2,000 years after his death.

"But Jesus called them to him and said, 'You know that the rulers of the world lord it over them, and their great ones exercise authority over them. It shall not be so among you. But whoever would be great among you must be your servant, and whoever would be first among you must be your slave, even as the Son of Man came not to be served but to serve, and to give his life as a ransom for many.'"
—Matthew 20:25-28 ESV

Absolutely Believe & Lead Greatly!

Chapter 2:
Culture

*Culture is the way one perceives the social
and behavioral characteristics of the group.*

Your business will have a culture, that is an absolute. Every business has a culture. Whether it's good, bad, or indifferent, they have one. The question is, will it be defined *by* you, or will it be defined *for* you?

You see, we all dream about what our business is going to be like in the future, and it's awesome! Everyone loves to work there! There's never any dysfunction! Everyone just does the right thing because they are adults! Everyone works hard, and we break all kinds of records because, well—it's just awesome!

I hate to break it to you, but it'll likely never be that utopian. We should strive for that utopia, and with the right strategies and tactics we might just become an awesome place to work.

If you, on the other hand, don't devise a strategy, you'll likely end up with something far from what you were dreaming of because the culture will be defined by the people in it, and one bad hire or strong personality can ruin a culture and a business in no time.

If you're already running a business, there's definitely a culture. There tend to be three fairly distinct groups when it comes to how they perceive the value of culture. First, there are a few contractors who have gotten on the culture bandwagon and developed some pretty great cultures. Then there are those that haven't gotten on that bandwagon but have a good culture. They likely are still small as a business and/or very lucky. The last group is the businesses that haven't bought into the value of culture and think it's a waste of time. They say things like, "We have sales to make and jobs to build, who has time for that?" Yet, they wonder why the good people that they hire slowly become lazy, and they are constantly dealing with turnover. It's because your culture sucks. Usually if your culture sucks, you need to take a look in the mirror and ask yourself if your leadership does too. Remember, each strategy builds off of the previous strategy.

Hiring people is expensive. To be exact, the average new hire in the U.S., costs a business approximately $5,000 just to hire and up to $50,000 dollars in training, limited production, and lost opportunity. Hiring great people costs even more! It's literally like flushing 500 $100 bills down the toilet every time we make a poor hire. If you like flushing money down the toilet, keep telling yourself that culture isn't a priority. On the other hand, if you like money—like I do—invest in building a great culture, or, more importantly, a powerful culture. It's so powerful that the best talent is attracted to it and wants to be a part of it! A powerful culture is a magnetic culture.

Let's get to work…

In our coaching, culture is broken down into five components, and yep, you guessed it, they happen in a specific order. You're probably going to get very tired of hearing that…

JIM JOHNSON

They are in a specific order because it is a goal. The goal is to have a great culture that everyone believes in and that is driven by the passion to be a part of it. Like any other goal, you have to start big and then break it down until it is believable and achievable. The five components of a great company culture are The Dream, The Vision, The Purpose, The Core Values, and finally The Mission.

The Dream

The Dream is an owner's responsibility and often not shared with anyone because of its personal nature—although we highly encourage it, if it's appropriate. Share it to people you trust and confide in. They will hold you accountable to achieving it.

As I stated earlier, we all dream about what our business will become, but it's usually pretty foggy, changes often, and is likely utopian. We just know it's going to be great and that's the last we think about it, if we thought about it at all. If we're honest with ourselves, our dream is usually something like this: I'm going to start my business, we're going to be the best at what we do, great people are going to work for me, and I'm going to make a ton of money, sell it for gobs more money, retire young and rich, and travel the world with my amazing better half! Simple enough. Now that it's done, what should I do today? And from that day forward, the furthest we think ahead is maybe a year, but usually more like a month or week—or even worse, tomorrow. With this type of approach, there is no ultimate goal or purpose behind our work. Taking this strategy will undoubtedly leave you directionless and "shooting from the hip," causing you to be reactive in day-to-day decisions, which results in a dream that will never be realized and a life that feels unfulfilled.

38

I want nothing more than to help you realize your dreams, and I hope they are far more powerful and life changing than the one above. ***Key Point:*** If we know who we are and why what we are doing fulfills us, we can develop a strategy to get there that will keep us focused on the ultimate goal. The likelihood of a dream or vision (which we'll talk about next) being achieved increases 70% when we write it down, share it with others, and refer back to it often with regular progress checks as compared to a 35% success rate when we keep them private[1].

What's your dream? I don't mean just the dream for your business but YOUR dream! For many of our clients, when we sit them down and really think about it, their business is really just the vehicle that gets them one step closer to achieving their ultimate dream. That is not to say that your business can't be a part of your dream or even your ultimate dream. I just want you to really think about it. Who are you? What brings you the most joy when you are doing it? If money was not a factor, what would you be doing right now?

This is by far the most important part of this book for you personally. It's not something we sit down and contemplate nearly often enough. Who are we? What is our purpose? Why are we doing all this in the first place? What impact will we have on our family, community, maybe even the world? What will your legacy be? This isn't just for owners—this is for everyone, and once you've done yours, I highly encourage you to teach others to do the same. A life without purpose is no life at all; it's simply going through the motions every day in an effort to just survive. I don't want people to just survive. I want them to thrive and enjoy the journey to the goal as much as, or possibly even more than, achieving the goal itself. Purpose applies meaning to our lives.

---

1   Study by Dr. Gail Matthews at Dominican University of California

Key Point: Meaning is the catalyst that turns the daily grind into the joyful grit that we need to persevere, regardless of the obstacles we face in pursuit of fulfillment.

The reality is that we all only have so much time on this planet. We don't know how long that will be. What are we going to do with that time, knowing that today could be that day? If it was today, what would people say about you at your funeral? How would they remember you? How long would they remember you? How long will your influence impact them and those that they come into contact with? Will that influence be passed onto future generations? What will your legacy be?

If your dream is to be happy, write down what happiness really is to you. If your dream is to have the biggest business in your industry, write down exactly what that means to you. If your dream is to have a massive impact of some type, write down what that is and how it will affect others.

Our clients' dreams are amazing! Providing clean water in Africa, establishing missions in India, Peru, and Africa, feeding the hungry in their communities, building free roofs for veterans and those in need, pet adoption, golden retrievers for children with cancer, growing new leaders, serving the underserved, and the list goes on and on and on. These businesses are using their business as the vehicle to shape the world around them in a positive way because of who they are. How will you change the world?

Before you take on this task, I'll share mine with you to give you an idea of what you're shooting for. It's usually just a high-level view—think 50,000 feet—and about two or three paragraphs.

My dream is to change the world from a selfishness, greed, and pride attitude to a serve-one-another attitude using connection through genuine love.

I will accomplish this by working with those I work with best, kids in middle and high school, who believe they can't because of their circumstance. I will show them that they can if they want something badly enough.

They will understand they can with the proper growth mindset, learned 7 Leadership Habits, creativity, hard work, and a servant heart. Through this, I will be doing God's work, for those who are willing and ready to listen, to find hope and salvation by leading in a Christlike way.

Three paragraphs, very high level, full of epic impact, and really not much to do with Contractor Coach PRO. Contractor Coach PRO is just one of the many vehicles along my journey that provides an opportunity to achieve my dream.

Now, I want you to close this book (never thought I'd say that as an author), and I want you to find a quiet place. Turn off your phone (I promise the world will not come to an end if you do) and have no TV, no music, no other people, no distractions of any kind. I want you to just think first. Close your eyes and develop a picture in your mind of what you see yourself doing when it is all said and done. What have you achieved? What impact did you have? What have you left behind as a legacy? What did you do to get there? Think big, don't hold back, and decide what you REALLY want to do with this gift of life you've been given. Then write it down, memorize it, make a copy, frame it, and place it where you'll see it every day—not for anyone else, just you. Take the other copy with you everywhere, and when you feel the stress, anxiety, or lack of focus of the world we live in closing in, pull it out, remind yourself why you're doing what you're doing, and get back on track.

The Vision

The Vision is where we combine The Dream with the business. We reel it back in to three years. What do you have to do with your business in the next three years to move you closer to your dream? This part of the culture process is for the owner and trusted key players that you know are in it for the long haul. Those who want to be a part of something powerful. Remember, this is still your business and your Dream, but by getting them involved you will gain that all important buy-in by showing them that they have a role in the ultimate goals of the business and that it will benefit themselves and others.

Unlike The Dream, where there is only one step, there is a step-by-step process for creating The Vision. Everything in your Vision must be qualified by your Dream. If it doesn't move you closer to realizing your Dream, it should not be included.

Again, whether you're doing this by yourself or with a small group of trusted leaders, you need to remove all distractions. Find a place that isn't your office, like a hotel conference room, a retreat facility, an Airbnb, or just that quiet place you use to get work done.

Let's get to work...

Step 1: What is possible?
What is possible for your business in the next three years? Don't hold back here. This should be an extensive list of every possibility you can think of for your business to achieve in the next three years. Is it possible to double, triple, or even 10X your revenue in the next three years? Is it possible to gain government contracts? Is it possible to go from residential—as the majority of your work is—

to commercial? Is it possible to hire 10, 20 or 100 new salespeople? It's it possible to get 1,000 5-star reviews? Is it possible to create 10,000 leads per year? Is it possible to create a charity or foundation? Is it possible to add a new niche(s) for your services? As you can see, the possibilities are endless. Write them all down!

Step 2: What's realistic and provides the most value? Strategic Intent
Strategic Intent is the term used to describe the aspirational plan, overarching purpose, or intended direction needed to reach an organizational vision. In other words, the ultimate goal(s) for your business over the next three years.

In Step 2, you (and your team) need to go through the list of possibilities and determine the ultimate goal that can actually be achieved in the next three years. These will be the highest aspirations and best direction for your business to focus on to achieve its Vision and, ultimately, your Dream. Here's we're the real struggle begins, especially when working with a team. Remember that you're using Leadership Habit #1, *Engage*, to connect with your team. Take your time here. Listen to your instincts, your internal voice, and the voices of your team. What out of all of these possibilities is likely to have the biggest impact on our business and our Dream? Do not be tempted to take on more than you can achieve. I assure you, you will—we are full of amazing ideas. Also, be cautious of taking on things that are too small and can be done in less than three years. We're trying to develop strategic intent here, not the individual strategies or tactics of that intent (we'll handle the strategies and tactics later in the mission).

For example, using the above list of all the possibilities, our strategic intent that is realistic and provides the most impact, while still pushing us, might be...

> *Strategic Intent:*
> *To increase our revenue by becoming a recruiting company that hires only the best team that is the best trained, wants to be a part of our amazing culture, and aspires to be the recognized leader in our market by becoming a service-first company. Once we have achieved this in our niche, repeat in similar niches.*

That is a huge strategic intent that could drive a business to explosive growth. It's so big it will take all of three years to achieve it, but if you are able to accomplish it sooner, you can create an opportunity for a new strategic intent to continue your growth.

Be careful not to get caught up in "how" you will execute your strategic intent. Like I said, we'll get to that later. Focus on what your possibilities are "saying" when you look at them all together.

If you look at the list above, it says that "recruiting," "becoming a service-first company," and "repeating" will provide the best opportunity for our business.

What is your business's strategic intent over the next three years?

Step 3: What does the environment of our business look like in three years?

The environment of your business is your culture personified. It is what anyone, either internally or externally, perceives your company to genuinely be like.

Once again, you are focused more on strategic intent than

how you will create the actual environment. It's hard to develop the strategies without knowing exactly what you intend for those strategies to accomplish. In other words, what do you intend the environment to be? We'll create the strategies and tactics to make it happen later in this chapter.

So, what type of environment do you intend to have? Will it be aggressive and/or competitive? Will it be calm and/or structured? Will it be more of a corporate feel or friends-and-family? Is it an "all for one, one for all" team, several small teams, or more "everyone's an individual" based? Will you all hang out together outside business or is business just business? Will you be active in the community or simply focused on your goals? Will you get all kinds of rewards and accolades, or do you want to stay under the radar?

As you can see, there are a lot of different environments, and I'm sure there are others that I haven't mentioned. The really cool part is that they can all be wildly successful because they fit the persona of the people involved. The problem arises when we don't determine what our environment will be; at some point, it will become dysfunctional because it doesn't align with everyone's values and personalities.

Think about it. If you're going for a "sportsy and competitive" environment for your culture where everyone is hanging out together, working hard, and playing hard, and you bring in a corporate, suit-and-tie, boring operations leader who doesn't want to mix business with their personal life, you just created dysfunction no matter how great they are at their job.

Determine your intended environment, we'll create the strategies to bring it alive. Then always—and I mean always—hire to that environment!

Step 4: Why are we doing it, and why do you believe in it? Purpose and Passion.

I learned a long time ago that if I really want someone to do something, they have to know why they are doing it and how it benefits them to do it. Remember, we're working on your Vision here, and the first habit of being an effective leader is to engage someone with your Vision. We are engaged by great stories. You will tell this story over and over again, and it will motivate, inspire, and drive them every time because of its purpose. They also play a role and are an important character of that story. When you share this Vision with someone for the first time, you'll know right away if they want to play a part in your story because their values and motivations align with your cause. You will see the excitement on their face and in their actions. A likely new teammate. If they don't, it will be as plain as if it were written on their forehead. Under no circumstances should that person be on your team. If you notice that no one wants to be a part of your story or that the only people who do are desperate, then your story is too much about you and not enough about them.

So, why? Why are you doing what you do? Why does it make a difference? Why can we do it better? Why are we focused on making an impact? Why do you make the world a better place?

One of the things I hear today that drives me crazy is, "the young people entering the workforce today just don't want to work." Those "lazy millennials." It's not that they are lazy, it's just that they are motivated differently than us more experienced—I refuse to say "older"—members of the workforce. The part I find humorous is that we taught them to be this way as our children. Think about it. Most of us leading in businesses today are Gen-X'ers. Our parents taught us that the world is a hard place, and we have to be hard. Nothing is given to you, it is earned. We have to start at the bottom and work hard to rise to the top and, even then, we probably won't make it or amount to much. They also instilled in us the "American Dream." A house, two cars, two kids, a dog, a white picket fence, save your money to retire and relax on the front porch and grow old together. Whether we liked that job or not was not important, only the end result was.

That was their dream. We wanted more because we were told we can't, so we went to work to prove everyone wrong and get more. Normally, we were doing a job we despised, but it paid well, so we could get more. The reality is that we did a pretty amazing job, and continue to do so, but we also realized something that was key. We weren't happy. This is when we started to teach our kids that they could do anything they set their mind to. That they should be kids while they can and enjoy it. We pushed them to be involved in everything to find out what made them happy. It was never about money or things—we had that for the most part. It was about following your dreams.

Now remember, we think they're lazy. The reality is that they aren't, they just aren't passionate about what they are doing for you. They aren't motivated by money as much as we used to be. They see the value in simplicity because they see the complexity and anxiety our work brings to our lives, and they want nothing to do with it. I know I'm making a gross stereotype, but I want to drive home a point. It's not about money and it never was. It's about fulfillment and meaning, and we find that through purpose. They just haven't found theirs yet.

I hope you're starting to see why culture is so important. People today want to know why they should work for you and how they will be happy doing so because they want their contribution to make a difference, and there are plenty of other options out there besides you to do so.

So, why are you doing what you're doing, and how does that benefit the people working for you, their families, and the families or businesses you serve?

Step 5: What will we do?
I told you we would get to the "how," and this is where we begin, with the "what." The first thing we need to do to determine our what, is to establish our *Primary Objectives*. The primary objectives that you will accomplish to achieve your strategic intents. Before you can say "how" you are going to do something, you have to define "what" you are going to do. We will get into more detail on how these strategies will be achieved with detailed strategies and tactics in The Mission at the end of this chapter.

These are your primary objectives that are part of your engaging Vision, which make it clear that there are goals that will come to fruition over the next three years.

Looking back at Step 2, you developed your strategic intent based on all the possibilities. "What" objectives do you need to accomplish to achieve it? Think about it as the primary objectives that will bring about your strategic intent. The goal is to be able to share an outline without your story becoming boring from too many details.

Here is an example:

> *Strategic Intent:*
> *To increase our revenue by becoming a recruiting company that hires only the best team that is the best trained and wants to be a part of our amazing culture.*

Primary Objectives:
1. *A recruiting process with a never-ending flow of new candidates.*
2. *A culture where everyone who fits wants to work forever because it is competitive, fun, and provides them an opportunity to achieve their goals.*
3. *Receive the top service awards in our industry, annually*
4. *Achieve $30 million in annual sales with a net profit margin of 12%*

Now the picture is getting a little clearer, and it's getting easier to see that we just might be able to pull this off!

Each of the objectives listed above would likely result in us achieving our Vision and Dream.
What will you do? What are your primary objectives?

The next thing we need to do in determining our "what" is to determine the *High-Level Strategies* that will be used to achieve our primary objectives and thus our overall strategic intent. Considering your primary objectives and strategic intent, what high-level strategies will we create to achieve the ultimate goal(s) of our three-year Vision? How can you leverage available resources to gain a sustainable advantage? What new resources might you need?

Here is a high-level strategy example based on the strategic intent and primary objectives:

High-Level Strategy:
1. *We will create an innovative sales process that makes buying easier. It will be strictly trained, provide our reps better success, and create happier customers.*
2. *We will create the best training program in the industry to retain our awesome team and ensure customer happiness.*

3. *We will provide tools, support, and benefits that our competitors don't offer to retain our awesome team.*
4. *We will dominate our market from a digital marketing standpoint to provide more opportunities to our team.*
5. *We will generate more leads by developing a powerful marketing strategy using innovative tactics.*
6. *We will develop a powerful culture to recruit only the best talent that loves working here.*

What are your high-level strategies to achieve your primary objectives and make your strategic intent a reality?

Step 6: What happens if we achieve our goals? Benefit. The climax of the story of your Vision! This is where we suck them in because opportunity abounds, and the reward is realized!

If you do what you set out to do, what opportunities does it create? Will you open new locations that need new leaders? Will you have new leadership positions that open up from your growth? Will there be additional benefits? Will there be an ownership opportunity? Will there be profit sharing or a company vacation? You get the idea— the opportunities are endless.

What about the reward for accomplishing your tasks? How many new leaders were created throughout the process? How many lives will you have improved by working for you? How many new jobs have you created? How much did your charitable initiatives accomplish? How many awards did you win?

Think of it as the payoff that you will constantly engage the team in and encourage the team to strive for, even in the face of adversity as you travel this journey.

What will happen if you achieve the goals of your Vision?

Step 7: Write your vision down!
Now that you have all the particulars of your Vision worked out, you NEED to write it down. Remember, you're 70% more likely to achieve it if you write it down and put it where you see it every day.

Take all the work you've done in Steps 2-6 and write it out as if it were a story or sales pitch. The reality is that this is what we are doing all the time with our team. Selling them the value of pursuing this Vision. The best sales situation is a win-win situation, and that is what your Vision needs to be.

Start with the strategic intent, or ultimate goal, of your Vision. Then explain what it will be like to work in your environment. Next, comes why you're doing it and why they might want to be a part of it. Now that they're interested, write what you'll get done together, and finally, how it will all pay off for everyone in the end.

Now you have an engaging Vision that like-minded, talented people will want to be a part of.

What is your Vision?

The Purpose

The next component of our Culture is The Purpose. Think of Purpose as your vision's rallying cry. ***Key Point:*** Purpose makes you and your team want to jump out of bed and crawl through glass to make it happen every day.

The *Purpose Statement* supplies the passion that drives the entire team. It is your "why." If you want to learn more about why your "why" is so important, I suggest you take the time to read the book *Start with Why* by Simon Sinek. Although I believe "who" before "why" is where we should start, understanding your "why" will completely change how you look at the purpose of your business and inspire others to be a part of it, whether as a teammate or as a customer.

A lot of our clients have had slogans and taglines that they hang their hat on. When asked if that gets anyone out of bed and excited to do it, the answer is usually a dismal "no." The answer has only been "yes" once. For that company, they knew their Purpose was to "Protect Families!" Not just the families they were providing services to, but the families of each of the team members. They accomplished this purpose not just through their work, but through various charitable initiatives for protecting families. As for our other clients, once they understand the role of Purpose to their company and the team, we help them go through the following simple exercise to develop theirs. This aspect of developing your Culture involves the entire team. So, while it's simple in the amount of steps, the difficulty lies in getting consensus from the entire team on why you do what you do. When our clients struggle gaining consensus, we step in as coaches and guide the exercise to ensure full buy-in.

Earlier, I said the most important part of this book for *you* was The Dream. Well, the most important part of this book for *your business* is The Purpose. At the end of the exercise, you'll know you've got it because it will be an "ah ha" moment. The volume will rise as you get closer and closer, and the excitement will reach a crescendo when people start yelling out, "That's it! That's why we do what we do!" Everyone else will be nodding their heads in agreement with smiles on their faces because who you are as a team is aligned with why you are doing what you do.

So let's get to work...

Step 1

Write down all the core words and phrases that describe your business. We suggest at least 25 but no more than 50. Remember these are "core" descriptions of your business. They normally start out with the standard stuff: quality, expertise, integrity, honesty, say what we do and do what we say, experience, being well trained, etc. Then they will start to get more creative: innovative, fun, technology driven, winners, etc.

It is key here for you as the leader to let the team roll first. You want to make sure they have time to express their own thoughts. However, you should also come prepared with your own words and phrases so you can guide the direction of the discussion. What you don't want to do is write down a bunch of purpose statements and then vote on them. If your team isn't involved, it'll end up just another tagline that no one believes in! In other words, if they aren't involved, there's no buy-in. I will say though, when you're first starting the business, it's an exercise you should do yourself. It gives you Purpose and will make sure that the people you show as you grow are aligned with you. After you get a few people and they've been there long enough to know they're on the team, sit down and do this exercise with them.

Now, as you're writing down the team's core words and phrases it is not uncommon to start out strong but eventually get stuck. You don't want to just put anything on there; your team needs to realize the importance of the word "core." They may need a little nudge from you, but when you see this happening, offer up one of the words or phrases that they haven't mentioned yet. This should spark a few more contributions from the group. Pay special attention to your list and how many of your words and phrases were already stated. If most of your list is gone, you and your team are on the same page. If you have a word or two that you feel needs to be added, offer them up for discussion. Each time you offer up a suggestion, do so with a question like, "What do you guys think about _____? Does that describe who we are at our core?" When you ask someone what they think, instead of telling them what to do, you are looking to them to have a real say in what The Purpose of the business will be. By asking in this manner, you get that all important buy-in, and once you define your Purpose, your teammates will feel like it was their idea after all.

Step 2

Sometimes after Step 1, you might not have enough words, or you need a few more "feel" words that add emotion to your purpose added to your list.

Ask the team what core words or phrases they want your customers and your community to feel about your company. This will spark a whole new discussion and set of words like: giving, experts, educational, caring, etc.

Purpose is all about feeling. It is emotional, inspiring, and exciting. If people love feeling those emotions, then you're building a powerful, magnetic culture!

Step 3

Now that you have a strong list of words and phrases, it's time to start mixing and matching them together to form statements. These statements should establish why you do what you do. They may initially start out as long, rambling statements in order to include everything. Write them down, even if they're a sentence or two long. We're shooting for three to eight words that describe you internally and externally. It's super important that it's memorable and evokes emotion.

For example, when I started Contractor Coach PRO, I wrote my own purpose statement: *Coaching Premier Contractors on How to WIN!* That statement got me out of bed and excited to help people like you do great things every day. As our team grew, we went through the exercise I just explained to you. After many alternatives, the team gravitated back to my original purpose statement. They asked if that was really why we do what we do. After a long conversation, it was paired down to its core: *Coaching Contractors to Win!* My team was right. We weren't coaching "premier" contractors, but we were coaching contractors who wanted to become premier. The word "how" in the original purpose statement was just wasted space. If they were winning, they were naturally learning how.

The goal is to get something to start with and reevaluate it every year, pairing it down to its core. If the problem is larger, and your purpose seems like it may no longer match your company, ask yourself if that is still your "why." The "why" can change over the years as you grow and realize there's more to your "why" than you originally thought. Ours has evolved to its current form—*Empowering People to Believe*—because that is why we do what we do. We empower contractors to believe in themselves and the strategies we help them develop to achieve their dreams. We empower those that work for us to believe that they are making an epic impact on an industry that makes the world a better place, and we empower all people to believe that there is a God, and he loves us all enough to sacrifice his perfect son for our salvation no matter how broken we are and will continue to be. Not by yelling it out on the street corners of our industry, but by our actions serving others.

That is a powerful statement! My team and I are excited to go out and do it every day because we've found the purpose in our work.

What's yours?

Step 4
Now that you have your purpose statement, it's time to make it your brand. This is the front facing part of your business that tells everyone why they should work with and for you. Make a sign and post it inside the front door of your office. Put it on all of your emails, include it in your marketing, and put it on your vehicles. In no time at all, people will start to say, "Oh you're the company that [insert purpose statement here]!" Establish your purpose and make it your brand. They will understand who you are and why you do what you do, and your brand will align them with you becoming your ideal client.

The Core Values

Core values (generally speaking) are the fundamental beliefs of a person or organization. These guiding principles dictate behavior and can help people understand the difference between right and wrong. Core values also help companies to determine if they are on the right path and fulfilling their goals by creating an unwavering guide for their behavior.

The Core Values of a business should ensure alignment with all who work there. If a person's core values are different from The Core Values you've set for your business, they most likely won't join your team. That's a good thing! A team aligned in The Purpose, The Core Values, and The Mission are significantly more likely to achieve The Vision, than a group that is not aligned.

I think the key word in the first paragraph on core values is "unwavering." Remember my story about firing one of our top sales reps because they weren't following our core value of "honesty"? I was unwavering. You will need to be too, so choose your Core Values wisely. ***Key Point:*** If you aren't willing to let someone go who isn't embodying or striving to embody a Core Value, then it isn't a Core Value.

Fortunately, most of your hard work for this portion of creating your Culture is already done. Remember all those core words and phrases you wrote down to develop your purpose?

Let's get to work...

Step 1
Take that list and make several copies. Have everyone vote on their top five. Tally up the scores, and boom, you should have three to eight Core Values that everyone agrees are the most important behaviors. Your teammates should understand that they will be held accountable to these values, and they should be willing to do so. As you create these Core Values, make sure not to use two words with similar meanings like "honesty" and "integrity." Choose the one that suits you and your team best. You'll have the opportunity to use the similar word when you do Step 2.

Step 2
Briefly describe what each Core Value means to your company. This could be a sentence or two to three bullet points. We do this to make sure that the word means the same thing to everyone. For example, if one of your Core

Values was "teamwork," that could mean different things to different people. One person may see teamwork as simply doing their job to support the team, while another would see it as being willing to do things outside their job duties to ensure the team's success.

Step 3

Now that we have our Core Values and they're all written down, place them front and center as a constant reminder to everyone of the behaviors they will be held accountable to. We've seen this executed in a variety of ways: posters for each Core Value all throughout the office, the Core Values themselves on the wall in the sales war room or training center, a plaque on the wall when you walk through the front door. The only wrong way to go about this is to not post them at all.

Here is an excellent example of a client's Core Values being posted as a reminder to the entire team[2].

---

2   If you want a copy of our Core Value posters to use as a template, you can download them at https://bit.ly/CCPcorevalues.

The Mission

This is where we are a little different from other coaches and consultants. This isn't a mission statement. You've already done that with your Purpose.

The Mission is more of a military mission. A mission to be developed by an owner and their management team. We have an objective to achieve in the next year that is aligned with The Core Values, The Purpose, The Vision, and The Dream.

Remember we started our "how" with Step 5 in The Vision by defining our "what." Now, we're going to put teeth into it by developing The Mission that defines "how" The Vision will be achieved. These are the specific strategies and tactics that will be used over the next year to achieve the high-level strategies of our Vision in the next three years. To complete this exercise, you will sit down with your key players and managers once a year to plan The Mission. Then, on a weekly, monthly, quarterly, and yearly basis, you and your team will review your progress, hold each other accountable, and make adjustments if necessary. At your yearly meeting, you will analyze the success or failure of your Mission and develop a new one. After three years, you should have achieved the high-level strategies, your primary objectives, and the strategic intent of your Vision and it's time to start creating The Vision for the next three years. The basic mission meeting template you downloaded earlier in the book will help you stay on track.

If you are familiar with military missions, then you know they start with the goal of the mission. They're given an operational name like "Desert Storm," then the specific strategies and tactics of the operation are decided on in order to execute the mission efficiently and effectively. Next, they determine the assets they'll need like tanks, artillery, planes, and soldiers. Last but not least, they define what success of the mission will look like if executed properly.

Key Point: We're going to do the same thing for our business, and your Mission will absolutely drive your Culture for the next year.

Step 1: What's the goal of your Mission?

One of the biggest mistakes we see here is developing The Mission that isn't in alignment with The Dream, The Vision, The Purpose, and The Core Values. You'll want to refer back to them as often as you develop your Mission. This step is necessary to hold yourself accountable to what you're really after and why you're doing what you're doing. If anything is suggested for The Mission that isn't in alignment with the rest of your Culture, it cannot be included.

So, let's refer back first to our Vision, specifically Steps 2 and 5 in developing the goal of our Mission. Here we find the strategic intent, primary objectives, and high-level strategies for our business over the next three years. What do we have to do this year to make that reality? What is your strategic intent saying you should do? What primary objectives must be achieved? What high-level strategies will you incorporate? Have an in-depth discussion with your leaders, and the goals of your operation should start to become clear.

I'll use the example from earlier in this chapter when we discussed Vision.

> *Mission Goal:*
> *To grow and expand our business by $(X) by becoming a marketing, recruiting, and service-first organization, not an [insert your specific trade or industry here] business.*

The $(X) of growth could be a third of the primary objective, but I like to shoot for the stars and hopefully land on the moon, so I would go for half. The first year is usually easiest for explosive growth, so let's ensure that we have a head start on years two and three.

If you really look at the strategic intent, primary objectives, and high-level strategies—the actual "work"—our example business does is just that, work. It doesn't matter what industry or trade they are in, they are choosing not to be defined by that. While this fictitious company does want to get better at quality, that will be covered by recruiting talented managers, foremen, and crews. What they really want to be is a recruiting, marketing, and service business. By doing this, they believe this approach gives them their best chance to succeed. It's in alignment with the Vision, so let's go for it.

What's the goal of your Mission?

Step 2: Name the operation.
By creating an operational name, you make it real and easier to communicate as the operation progresses. Just like with Desert Storm, we knew immediately what was being talked about, and we were riveted by its progress every time it was mentioned. Operation Enduring Freedom (The Afghan War), on the other hand, just didn't grab our attention in the same way. I personally couldn't remember the name of the operation and had to look it up. Your Mission must grab the attention of everyone on the team, so give it a great name. With our clients, we've had some great operational names. Operation Domination, Operation Serve the Underserved, Operation Sniper, Operation Ninja, Operation Organization, and the list goes on. Feel free to share your operational name in the "Work On IT, Not IN

It" Facebook Group! We'd love to hear them.

Step 3: Strategies & Tactics
Are we going to have a full- frontal assault? A sneak attack? Are we going to flank our opponent? How about a little "shock and awe"?

The strategies and tactics we use are paramount to the success or failure of any mission. While we don't suggest looking at your competition as "the enemy," they are still your competition. Your ultimate competition should be yourself. If you focus your Mission on you and what your team is doing, rather than what the competition is doing, your Mission has a much greater chance at success.

So, what are tactics and how are they different from strategies?

Chinese General Sun Tzu described the difference this way:

"All the men can see the tactics I use to conquer, but what none can see is the strategy out of which great victory is evolved."
—General Sun Tzu

Strategy is what's going on behind the scenes, while tactics are front and center. It's why people can copy our tactics and never achieve what we achieve because they don't know how it relates to the overall strategy.

For example, our competition can see that writing a book is a tactic our company is implementing. But even if they read the book, which they will, they have no clue how it plays into our overall strategy. They can go write books to their heart's content and never achieve the results we will because they can't see the overall strategy until it's too late.

In the contracting world, everyone can see your marketing ads, but they don't know how it plays into your overall recruitment strategy. They can see your entire sales presentation but don't realize how it works in relation to your community impact strategy. They can see the ads you run to recruit great talent but don't know how that is just a piece of your Culture strategy.

It's one of the best things I have learned in my life, and I learned it by reading *The Art of War* by Sun Tzu. ***Key Point:*** We can share all the tactics we have with every competitor, and they'll still never be able to replicate our success because they don't see the strategy the tactic is designed to achieve.

In Step 5 of The Vision exercise that you did earlier, you listed out the high-level strategies you would use to achieve your primary objectives and strategic intent. Referring back to those, what strategies and tactics will you implement to accomplish these high-level strategies?

Let's do an example from our earlier work with our fictitious company to give you an idea of what it should look like...

> *Mission Goal:*
> *We will create an innovative sales process that makes buying easier. It will be strictly trained to our teammates by our leaders, provide our reps more opportunity for success, and produce happier customers.*
>
> *Strategies & Tactics:*
> 1. *We will create an in-home presentation and demonstration (tactic) that walks customers through the buying process based on their choices with our expert guidance*

(tactic) so that the logical choice in the end is to choose us, virtually eliminating all objections (strategy).
2. *We will train every day on mastering our sales process (tactic) to ensure we get better everyday (strategy).*
3. *We will hire a Customer Happiness Expert (tactic) to ensure customer happiness (strategy) through a well-trained follow-up system (tactic).*

Now that you get the idea, what are the tactics you will use to achieve your high-level strategies? Discuss with your leadership team, and—really, at this point I shouldn't have to say this, but—WRITE THEM DOWN!

Now you should have all your strategies and tactics for the first year for each of your high-level strategies that relate to each strategic intent of your business.

Step 4: You'll Need Assets.
In order to achieve the goal of your Mission, you're going to need a few assets. Unless you're just made of money, you need to determine the right asset to execute any particular tactic efficiently and effectively.

For example, you want to double the number of leads you're getting. You could go out and spend bookoo bucks on a high-powered marketing firm. Is that in the budget? Would they be any more effective than if you just ramped up your referral program?

Choose your assets wisely for each one of your tactics.

Let's go back to our fictitious company's strategies and tactics and do one together so you nail your assets!

Strategy and Tactic #1:
We will create an in-home presentation and demonstration that walks customers through the buying process based on their choices with our expert guidance so that the logical choice in the end is to choose us, virtually eliminating all objections.

Assets We Need:
1. *An outline of our sales process based on the best practices of our current team*
2. *A list of objections so we can address them proactively in our presentation*
3. *A unique offering to separate us from our competition that creates value to eliminate the price objection*
4. *A digital presentation*
5. *A demo case*
6. *An app to show the finished project before we start to get the get emotion into the sale*
7. *A leader to take on this project and test it until it's proven*

As you can see, some of our assets could be an even more detailed strategy or tactic in order to execute our Mission. A *Digital Presentation* is an *Asset* that you will need to complete your Mission, but it is also a tactic you will use instead of a Flip Book or Verbal Presentation, like your competition.

Yep, it's that time again. What *assets* will you need to execute the *strategies* and *tactics* to accomplish your mission?

With these assets, we should start to realize that accomplishing The Mission is actually achievable, in turn making it more likely to realize The Vision, which brings us one step closer to The Dream.

Step 5: Define what success looks like in the end, today!
This tends to be the most difficult part of The Mission. People tend to be too analytical and have a hard time defining what success of a Mission looks like. It usually looks something like this...

> *Our mission will be successful if we hit this number in revenue and generate this number of leads, with this number of reps closing at this percentage.*

Good grief, could that be any more boring?!

This part of the Culture exercise isn't one-for-one (i.e., if we do this then it will make this specific part of our mission successful). In other words, success isn't necessarily defined by accomplishing a strategy or tactic. It is part of the success, but you need to look at the big picture. Think about the cause and effect of your Mission.

Think about the impact your Mission will have if it is accomplished. All of the lives it will have changed, all of the opportunities it will create, all of the headaches it alleviated, how it got you closer to your Vision and Dream. That is a successful Mission.

What's your definition of success for your Mission?

As you can see, building a culture is a lot of work, and it never stops unless you allow it to. If you allow the pursuit of your defined culture to fall by the wayside, then you will no longer be defining it, circumstances and others will do that for you.

If you have done what we hoped you would by completing this exercise, you will have created a blueprint for your culture. This blueprint can serve you for years to come if you consistently reinforce it. On the other hand, if you end up putting it in a drawer somewhere, never to be seen again, then it was the biggest waste of time you'll ever have in your business. The secret to culture is to feed it and feed it often until it becomes a habit.

There's that word again, *habit*. You can't just write all of this down, announce it like it's law, and expect everyone to just jump on board. You have to use those 7 Leadership Habits to live your culture.

Engage your team with your Vision and remind them often. *Educate* them on The Vision, The Purpose, The Core Values, and The Mission. Set the *example* daily by being what you want them to be. Have *empathy* for them if they don't get it or buy-in right away. There's a lot of fear with anything new. *Encourage* them by recognizing their contributions to The Vision and The Mission and living The Purpose and The Core Values. *Empower* them by giving them tasks or projects they can handle to move the Mission forward. Finally, *expect* them to meet the standards you've set together as a team for your company culture.

In the leadership schedule you did in Chapter 1, you should have blocked time to engage, educate, empathize, encourage, empower, and inspect what you expect. If you paid close attention to the previous sentence, you'll notice I left out one of the seven Leadership Habits: example. You will be the example by blocking time for the other six. Through your example, others will start to believe in your Culture and begin to make it a habit too. Those are the ones who are bought in and are likely your future leaders. They will make your Culture contagious. They are your Culture Champions!

Here's just a few other ways to make your Culture contagious:
- Find a Culture Champion (if you aren't one)
- Give out Core Values awards
- Incorporate a Core Value assessment in your reviews
- Recognize people in meetings
- Have a weekly mission meeting
- Give ownership to projects and tasks with due dates and hold people accountable to them
- Have a quarterly strategy meeting to measure and analyze your progress on your Mission
- Randomly ask teammates what The Purpose and The Core Values are. Reward them when they get them right
- Have a yearly "Purpose Warrior" award

Be creative and work hard to reinforce your Culture. It will bear fruit sooner than you think if you feed it.

A final note on Culture.

You need to understand your *Secret Sauce*. These are the ingredients and recipe that define your business and give it its unique identity.

What are the key ingredients that make your business different and great? How do you mix those ingredients together to create something no one has ever "tasted" before?

Sometimes this is a difficult thing to see. It's why I believe so strongly in taking time away from your business to meditate and really think about it. It gives you an opportunity to see it for what it really is.

It actually took us a while to figure out our secret sauce here at Contractor Coach PRO, even though it was right in plain sight all the time.

I'll share the sauce with you, but the ingredients and recipe are—for the time being—a secret. If I told you, well you know, you had better have your head on a swivel.

Our secret sauce is… (drumroll please!) personal one-on-one coaching. It means getting in the trenches with you and creating a genuine relationship with you. It is not just about the strategies for your business, but the strategies for your life. It's what makes us unique.

Sometimes it's easier to see the sauce and then figure out the ingredients and recipe by reverse engineering.

Key Point: The best part about learning your secret sauce is discovering what ingredients to double, triple, or add tenfold when you need to feed a lot of people.

Things you can do now to improve your Culture:
1. Do the Culture exercise (above)
2. Include time in your leadership schedule to reinforce your Culture
3. Find a Culture mentor or coach
   • Seek out businesses in other trades or industries and ask to be mentored on culture if they have a great one
   • Hire a coach who can help you execute a winning culture strategy

> **"Customers will never love a company until the employees love it first."**
> **—Simon Sinek**

I'll end this chapter with another small piece of advice from the Good Book and the greatest Culture creator of all time:

"And Jesus came and said to them, 'Go therefore and make disciples of all nations.'"
—Matthew 28:19

Who will the disciples of your business be, and what will they follow?

Chapter 3: Process

Imagine a world where everyone in your company knows exactly what they are supposed to be doing, when they are supposed to do it, how to do it, what tool to use to do it with, and how that task relates to all the tasks before and after it. Wouldn't that be an awesome world? Imagine all the happy people working in that world. Imagine all the happy customers experiencing that world. Imagine all the happy leaders in that world. Thankfully, it is not an imaginary world. It is a world where Process, or standard operating procedures, exist. That world exists for huge corporations, but for home services contractors and most entrepreneurs, it is a rarity. It isn't just a process world, it is a written process world, and you have the power to make that imaginary world a reality. It does involve some heavy lifting, but once it is done, life gets so much easier!

Process is like algebra to me, I understand it's value, and I can see the steps in my head, but getting it down in written form—uggggh, kill me now! I imagine that many of you are like me when it comes to a written process. If so, you need to understand how process plays a vital role in the strategy of your business and there is no choice other than to do the dirty work and get it down in writing. The goal of this chapter is to share my strategy with you and make it a bit easier for you to accomplish. It is like eating an elephant, we can do it, but only one bite at a time.

The real value of Process isn't in the process itself, it's in the ability to share that process with everyone else so it is clearly communicated and repeatable. Having clearly-communicated Processes makes your business scalable and valuable, while greatly reducing the number of daily questions you need to answer. The biggest mistake I see is that we feel we need the *perfect* Process. Wrong! You need a *working* Process! Don't get me wrong, we should strive to get it perfect, but that feeling of needing to get it perfect, stops us before we even get started. The task becomes even more daunting if you're waiting until it's perfected to start. Let's start with getting a Process down in writing. Once that works, then strive to perfect it.

This isn't anything new I'm sharing with you. You know you haven't written down your processes, and if you have, you know that it is far from tight. You also know if you'd just take the time to get your processes written, you could stop 80% of the questions you get asked by your team. You don't have to be the Google Search Engine of your industry; let your process do it for you. The goal is to provide your team with a way to search for the answers they need without you being the sole resource. A written process accomplishes that.

I remember the day I finally decided to write down our Process. It was the same day I decided we needed a better training program. These two changes made a massive difference in the amount of time available to me, giving me more capacity to work on my business instead of in it.

It had been another long, hard day at the office of recruiting new reps, running training classes, and answering question after question up until about 11pm. (That was back before the days of the leadership schedule and me setting standards. Unfortunately, I hadn't learned that yet.)

Then it happened. A rep called me at 1:30am and asked, "Am I supposed to list the felt before or after the shingles on my order? And how many squares does a roll of 15# felt cover again?"

I think it was the word "again" that was the straw that broke the camel's back. I didn't even answer the question. I slowly pressed the "end call" button and proceeded to throw my phone across the room, shattering it to pieces. Well, at least no one else could bother me that night.

Unfortunately, I couldn't sleep. I tend to ask the question "why?" a lot. It's both a blessing and a curse, but when something isn't going the way I want it to or I think it can be done better, I start asking "why?" and sometimes "why not?" This has caused a lot of sleepless nights in my lifetime, as my amazingly understanding wife knows only too well. It's like that algebra question that needs to be solved. Asking those questions often has brought clarity to a situation, and often that clarity is that I am part of the problem. I can guarantee that if you are dealing with chaos and stress, the decisions you have made up to this point are part of the problem. The great thing is we can do something about it!

This night in particular, I started asking myself, "Why did that rep think he could call me at 1:30 in the morning?" The answer is, "because something I'd done had made him think it was ok." Why doesn't he know that felt comes after the shingles on all of our orders? I know I've told him at least a dozen times, and I know I covered it in detail in his training. Because that's not the way he learns, or that wasn't as important to him as the sales stuff that he's pretty good at. Why in the hell was he filling out an order at 1:30am? Because he's sold quite a bit, hasn't learned how to manage his time, and he's OCD, so he wants everything to be perfect. Yep, that's probably another reason he called. It went on like that for hours, and I came to three conclusions. First, our process wasn't clear enough for the size of our company. Second, we needed a better training program that didn't just get you started, but that reinforced early learning while giving constant continuing education. We had to get better every day. Third, I had to be better.

At the time, I didn't realize I was doing things to increase my capacity and exercising my leadership habit of empathy (I hadn't learned this yet either). I was simply solving a puzzle. I was developing strategies to allow me more time and putting myself in other people's shoes. If I could stop 80% of the questions that I got on a daily basis, what could I do with all that extra time? What were we giving our team that our competitors didn't offer? How would this make their jobs easier to learn, thus making them more successful right away? If I just put the time in now, the benefit in the future would be business- and life-changing.

I started that night—I was awake anyway. What I realized was that the format I came up with for creating a Process that night had been in my head the whole time. Just like that algebra equation, I had the answer but couldn't explain how I got there. I wasn't showing my work. If they could see how the Process worked on paper, they wouldn't have to continually ask me how and when to get things done.

Key Point: So, the most important thing you need to understand about developing a Process is that it is linear. In other words, it is a step-by-step method to get from point A to point B. The part most people fail to realize is that any deviation from that Process becomes a whole new procedure. Most people try to include that deviation in the Process, which starts a whole path of "if *this*, then *that*." However, if someone has to think about it, then you don't have a Process—you have a puzzle.

With our clients, we start with the job process for a specific trade in most cases, unless two different trades or multiple trades are treated as one job and follow the *exact* same process. We take it from initial contact to final payment, paperwork, and close-out. We call it the *Ideal Process*. Any deviation from the perfect job process is a new process. Once we coach them through building the ideal process, they now have the skill to create a Process for any deviations, trades, or other processes they may need. This applies not only for the business but for everything. I want to share that with you today. Let's stop the questions, let's make your business scalable, let's make your company valuable, and most of all, let's create more time—and thus more capacity—for you to work on your business. Last but not least, whether you use the following strategy or another, you must have a written process for everything.

I bet you know what's coming next...

Yep, there's an order to all things in the *Contractor's Blueprint*, and Process is no different. As a matter of fact, it's a process, like everything else, that has an order of operation. The *Contractors Blueprint* strategy is a Process. In other words, there's a process for building a Process!

Let's get to work...

Let's start with the ideal process, and then you can create other processes for any deviations, trades, or other necessary processes for your business from there. We like to use a spreadsheet for this, but you can use any tool that works best for you: a Word document, Google Docs, a pen and paper—I don't care. Just get it down in writing. Do, however, make sure you follow the format. We will give instructions as if you are using a spreadsheet, because we've found them to be the easiest to update quickly[1].

Step 1: Determine what roles are involved in your process - *Sheet 1, titled "Roles"*
This serves two purposes. First, it will identify everyone involved in the process, what they are doing, and when. Second, it comes in handy for the next chapter on Organization and HR for "Job Descriptions," but we'll refer back to this later in that chapter.

A couple of notes when considering the roles for your ideal process:

- Do not include "owner" as one of your roles. The whole purpose of this book is to get you working on it, not in it. There are rare occasions where an owner still wants to be involved in the Process, but do not use "owner" as a role. For example, one of our clients still wants to do the final inspection on every project they complete. The thing is, he's not doing that as an owner, he's really taking on the roles of Quality Control, Final Inspector, or Project Manager/Supervisor/Coordinator. Someday, they may have so much business that he can't physically do them all anymore, But someone will, and I promise you that that person's role won't be "owner."
- Remember, this is the process you *want* to follow, it's most likely not the process you *currently* follow. Therefore, you should include all the roles you can foresee being needed as your company grows. A current teammate may already be wearing two, three, or more hats. You most likely are. So make sure you account for those new roles the best you can before

---

1 If you'd like to download our template, you can do so at https://bit.ly/CCPprocess.

you need them. That way, you're not constantly having to update your Process. Just make sure the person performing more than one role knows which ones they are responsible for in your Process. They'll also be super pumped that you're planning ahead for their future.

- List the current roles being performed in your business first, then the future ones. Do this row by row if you're using a spreadsheet. This will make them easier to identify when you make a future role a current role.
- A role is not someone's name, it is a job title. Don't list your Office Manager as "Suzy" or "wife/husband." Suzy may not be there forever, and your wife/husband may not always be the Office Manager.
- Pay special attention to the titles you bestow on people. As I said before, words are powerful things, and certain words bring with them certain expectations for responsibility and compensation. I can assure that you, an Office Manager will want to be paid more than an Administrative Assistant but less than an Executive Administrator. Similarly, a Sales Manager will expect to be paid more than a Sales Team Leader but less than Vice-President of Sales. They're going to be looking for that nice, fat salary that's more than a Sales Manager. What I'm trying to get across is to not be cheap. Pay well and fairly for the true responsibilities and results of the role. Like I told anyone making big bucks at my company, those big bucks come with big responsibility, and they would be held accountable. One last thing on the name of your roles: be creative. "Customer Experience Expert" sounds way cooler than "Customer Service Rep" or "Account Manager," and it doesn't come with any compensation expectations, leaving you with flexibility.
- Finally, apply an acronym to each role. If you're using

a spreadsheet, use the next column to the right of the roles to list the acronym for the role. For example, "SM" for Sales Manager or "CEE" for Customer Experience Expert.

It took me more time to write this than it should take you to define your roles. You know the drill. Write them down. It should look something like Figure 3.1 when you are finished.

Roles	Acronym
General Manager	GM
Sales Manager	SM
Production Manager	PM
Office Manager	OM
Admin Assistant	AA
Customer Service	CS
Marketing Specialist	MS
Bookkeeper	BK
Project Manager	PMR
Sales Rep	SR
Estimator	ES
Future	
Business Development	BD
Marketing Manager	MM
Quality Control Specialist	QCS
Certified Inspector	CI
Accounts Payable	AP
Accounts Recievable	AR

Figure 3.1

Step 2: Determine your milestones - *Sheet 2, titled "Milestones"*

If you're currently using a Customer Relationship Management (CRM) software, it is likely that it has pre-determined milestones for clients and their jobs as they move through your process. Unless your CRM is fully customizable, ignore these milestones. They rarely are the actual milestones your clients go through. Most of the time, your jobs go through multiple milestones inside of their high-level ones. On the other hand, if yours is customizable, refer to the ones you've created but keep an open mind because you're building the process you want, not necessarily the one you have. You can add or subtract any milestones from your current Process in the CRM when you're done.

It's at this point that we get some pushback from some of our clients, and I assume we'll get the same from those of you reading this book.

"My CRM is fully customizable. Our Process is already done." Yeah, sure it is. ***Key Point:*** Unless the process in your CRM explains exactly how and when to set up your ladder, what to do when you get a new lead, when to ask "objection defeating questions" in your sales process, or what questions to ask, how to ask them, and why, then your Process is incomplete.

Don't get me wrong, Process automation is an absolute must in today's fast-paced, technology-centered world. We'll get to that at the end of this chapter and even more in the chapter on Technology. But realize that you can't automate everything. Unless you like answering a million questions over and over, you must have a detailed written process.

Lecture complete. Now back to work.

The common milestones we see in the clients we work with look something like this:
1. Lead
2. Appointment
3. Pre-Inspection Presentation
4. Inspection
5. Presentation/Demo
6. Contract
7. Submit for Production
8. Pre-Production Review
9. Order
10. In Progress
11. Complete
12. Final Inspection
13. Invoice
14. Paid
15. Final Paperwork
16. Job Close-Out
17. Closed

Although our clients tend to be facing common issues, each client we work with has something unique about the milestones in their ideal process. They may be in a different order or have different names. Some have more, and some have less. The beauty of it is that they all work because it's a process they believe in and it is written down.

What are your milestones for your ideal process?

List your milestones by row on Sheet 2. It should look something like Figure 3.2 on the next page when you are finished.

Milestones
Marketing
Lead
Prospect
Inspection
Presentation
Prepare for Production
Ready for Production
In Progress
Completed
Close Out
Closed

Figure 3.2

Step 3: Sheet for each milestone

For each milestone you have created, you will want to create a sheet in your master spreadsheet. If you're working in a Word document or on paper, each milestone will have its own page.

At the top of the sheet, title it with the name of your milestone.

Then starting from the left below the title make five columns and give them the following titles:

Task	Condition	Tool	Role	Time

Copy the column titles and go to the next sheet. Title it and paste in the column titles. Repeat this process for the remaining milestones.

It should look similar to Figure 3.3 when you are done setting up your format.

Lead				
Task	Conditions	Tool	Role	Time

Figure 3.3

Step 4: Milestone tasks

Now starting with the first milestone, close your eyes and walk through the exact process for that milestone in detail, as if you were actually doing it. Focus on just the tasks and the order in which they happen and then list them step-by-step and row-by-row under the "task" column. Don't get into detail. That's what the "conditions" column is for. Think of it as the title of the task, or how you would say it to one of your teammates. We highly encourage enlisting the help of your team when building your Process, especially the ones that are performing the actual duties for that milestone. Several of our clients finish this part of the *Contractor's Blueprint* by having the team member responsible for that milestone fill it out. Make sure you inspect what you expect by reviewing their work and challenging them on the details.

For example, if your first milestone is "lead," then your first task might be "lead call." Your next task might be "follow lead call script." Your next task might be "set appointment," and so it goes, task-by-task, until the milestone is complete. Don't worry about scenarios beginning with "what happens if…" That's a deviation. Remember, we're building the ideal process as if everything is going according to plan. The only reference you might make is, "if X happens refer to the X Process." If you include a link to that process, they can quickly reference it and follow that process to its end.

Repeat this procedure for each milestone until complete. Do not fill out the other columns until you have completed all the tasks in each milestone. There are two reasons for this. One, by doing just the tasks first, you will have a process quicker than you can begin to use right away with your team. Two, if you need to add or remove a task as you are building your process, having the other columns filled out makes the whole process more difficult. Let's get the order right, then we can handle the "conditions," "tools," "role," and "time" columns for each.

Note: As you create the tasks and the conditions in the next step for each milestone, it helps to close your eyes, or even better, do it live with an actual job. No detail is too small! Don't skip something because you think everyone should just know that! Complete your tasks as if you hired a new person—a 7th grader—and they had to do the job without any guidance from a teammate.

When you are done it should look something like Figure 3.4 on the next page.

Lead		
Task	Conditions	Tool
Create Lead		
Assign Lead		
Mark Lead as Contacted		
Convert to Prospect		

Figure 3.4

Step 5: Conditions

Ok, you've worked hard and have gotten all the tasks for your process completed. Congratulations! That elephant is starting to disappear one bite at a time!

Some of the tasks you've created will be self-explanatory, but others will need some clarification. That's where the conditions come into play. The conditions make your process so clear that the 7th grader we hired earlier can follow it.

Be wary of thinking things like, "that task is obvious. It doesn't need any further explanation." It probably does.

For example, we'll use a task I mentioned earlier: "Set up ladder." While that may seem pretty cut-and-dry, the reality is that there is some pretty significant instruction that you need to be given. What feels like innate knowledge probably isn't to someone who is new to the job.

The condition for "Set up ladder" might look something like this.

> *Condition:*
> *Place the base of your ladder on a firm dry surface. Place the top of your ladder in a valley or low pitch area of the roof. Tie off your ladder and keep three points of contact with the ladder at all times for safety.*

There's probably more there that you could add from the OSHA safety handbook. The point is that the devil is in the details.

Now, carefully consider each task, in order, and determine if it needs further clarification or not. If the condition requires some explanation on using a technology or tool that you use, make sure to use the general reference for it. For example "CRM" rather than the specific name. We will do that in the "tool" column. This makes it quick and easy to update your process if you decide to switch tools in the future.

Now, go milestone-by-milestone and then task-by-task until all your conditions are complete.

Once you're finished, communicate with your team that the Process has been updated. Meet with them about it. Make any changes you may need based on reasonable suggestions from the team. Get agreement that this is your Process, and it will be followed to make everyone's life easier. You just eliminated the majority of questions.

It should look something like Figure 3.5.

Lead		
Task	Conditions	Tool
Create Lead	Use CRM to create the lead with Name, Address, Phone, Email, and Source of Lead	
Assign Lead	If generated by the office	
Mark Lead as Contacted	Upon setting an Appointment	
Convert to Prospect	Click "Convert to Prospect" button on the lead pace in CRM	

Figure 3.5

Step 6: Tools

As you've done in the previous step, you will be going through each milestone and its tasks in order and defining the tool to use when performing a particular task.

Once again, not every task will require a tool. In this column, use the specific name of the tool so anyone reading the process knows exactly what to use to perform the task.

Ready, set, GO!

It should look similar to Figure 3.6.

Conditions	Tool	Role
Use CRM to create the lead with Name, Address, Phone, Email, and Source of Lead	Job Nimbus	
If generated by the office	Job Nimbus	
Upon setting an Appointment	Job Nimbus	
Click "Convert to Prospect" button on the lead pace in CRM	Job Nimbus	

Figure 3.6

Step 7: Roles

At this point, you should have all of your tasks, conditions, and tools defined for your process. In this next step, we will once again be going through each task in every milestone in order. Using the acronym you created from the roles you defined earlier in your ideal process, assign the appropriate role to each task that performs it. Unlike in the "conditions" and "tools" columns, every task will have a role.

Upon completing this step, everyone should know what

needs to be done, when it should be done, how to do it, what tool to use, and who is doing it.

At this point, you have eliminated 80% of the questions you would normally have to answer on a daily basis.

Update the team that the Process has been completed. Call a company meeting for everyone that the Process involves and train them on it. Invite questions, make any justifiable edits, add any clarification on the conditions if necessary, and get everyone's agreement that this is THE ideal process. With that agreement, we can now hold people accountable to our Process.

Wait! Isn't there a fifth column for "time"? You are absolutely correct, and although it is the final step in building your ideal process, it isn't important to the actual functionality of the process or how it works. Let's get everyone using it, and Step 7 becomes more accurate.

Upon completing all of the roles, it should look like Figure 3.7.

Tool	Role	Time
Job Nimbus	JR/SR/Admin	
Job Nimbus	SM	
Job Nimbus	SR	
Job Nimbus	SR	

Figure 3.7

Step 8: Time
The beauty of a process is that it is something that can be measured. As we all should know by now as business

leaders, "what gets measured, gets improved"[2]. ***Key Point:*** In other words, if there is a "score" for something, it has been proven in dozens of studies that our basic human nature is to improve that score. Remember, this is the *ideal* process. Improving the score breeds a culture of continual improvement that strives to perfect the Process.

In the chapter on Accountability, we will be introducing you to the concept of *Velocity*. If a process is how you get from point A to point B, velocity is how fast you are getting from point A to point B. The faster you get there without sacrificing quality, the more volume you can handle, and the more profitable each job becomes. Like I said, we'll get more into that in the Accountability chapter, but for now we need some form of measurement to start with. This begins by assigning an amount of time that each task should take to complete.

Similar to the "roles" column above, each task needs to have a measurement of time associated with it. At this point in our Process building, we want to put in an amount of time that we want that task to take, not necessarily how long it is currently taking.

Some examples of time measurement we commonly see are:
- Immediately
- Minutes
- Hours
- Days
- Weeks
- Months (We hope nothing takes that long, but in some industries, it is unfortunately what we deal with. Especially in commercial or insurance restoration.)

---

2   This quote originates from Peter Drucker's book, *The Practice of Management*. The actual quote is, "What gets measured, gets managed."

When we add up the time for all tasks in each of the milestones, we will have a pretty good starting point for your ideal velocity.

It's that time again. Go through each task and associate a measurement of time with it. You may need the assistance of your team to get an idea of how long each task takes, but I assure you it's worth the effort to be as accurate as possible at this point.

Once again, when you're done, meet with the team and go through the completed Process with an emphasis on time. Make any adjustments that may be necessary and get agreement that it can be done. Encourage your team to come to you at any time you're available in your leadership schedule if they see a way to shorten the amount of time of the Process.

Your finished ideal process could look something like Figure 3.8 on the next page.

Whew! You did it! Step-by-step and one bite at a time! You ate the elephant!

Congratulations! You're well on your way to working on your business, not in it! Do your happy dance, recognize your team for their contributions, thank them for their effort, and celebrate a little.

"But all things should be done decently and in order."
—1 Corinthians 14:40

Lead

Task	Conditions	Tool	Role	Time
Arrive on time for Appointment	Minimum 5 minutes early		SR	5 minutes
Park in the street	Do not block driveway unless it is a long driveway to the home		SR	Immediately
Set up light s and cones	Set up the "show" of your inspection		SR	1 minute
Slam door	Draw attention to your inspection		SR	Immediately
Survey property for F.O.R.M.	Family, Occupation, Recreation, Motivation warm up talking points		SR	Immediately
Perform warm up	Using one of the F.O.R.M. components, initiate a conversation with the prospect		SR	5-10 minutes
Ask Objection Defending Questions	Used to eliminate possible objections during your presentation	See Training Manual	SR	5-10 minutes
Start Part 1 of		Tablet	SR	Immediately
Company Credibility	Slides 1-8		SR	3 minutes
Personal Credibility	Upon completion of company credibility. Make sure to include your training, certifications, and personal info (where you grew up, where you live, married or not, kids, hobbies, etc.). The goal is to start a conversation to built rapport. Become a friend, not a sales person		SR	1 minute
Inspection Expectations	Slides (-). Explain what you will be doing during your inspection, what they will receive, and how long it will take		SR	2 minutes
Million $ Walk-Around	Become the expert by pointing out damage, issues, and specific components that may be of issue.		SR	5 minutes
Do Your Homework	Ask the prospect to check your company out while you perform the inspection. Ideally, send them an email with your Reviews and Testimonial links attached to the correct button representation. For example, use the "Facebook Reviews," "Google Reviews," and other testimonial application links and link them to the logo buttons in a template email to send to each prospect while you are inspecting the roof.		SR	20-30 minutes

Figure 3.8

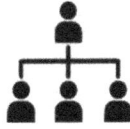

Chapter 4:
Employee Performance
(a.k.a. Organization & Human Resources)

At this point, you are probably starting to see a shift in the attitude of your team. You're becoming a stronger leader and they are seeing it. Your culture is still in its infancy, but there's a noticeable change for the better, and everyone feels like things are getting more organized and streamlined, making everyone's jobs easier. We're well on the way to scaling your business, but this is just the foundation. Your business needs a framework to support that growth, and that's where Organization and Human Resources comes in to optimize employee performance.

The larger your company grows, the harder it becomes to directly communicate with your team, which is why it is so critical to have clearly-defined policies and procedures in place. By ensuring that they are not only defined—but written down and shared with the team—you are also scaling your ability to communicate with all current and future team members and reducing one of the big headaches that can come with growth.

One of the biggest mistakes we see in companies when we begin to work with them is policies and procedures being verbally communicated instead of documented in writing. When we verbally communicate information, what we say to one teammate might not be exactly what we tell another teammate. Although they don't mean to, I've also seen owners give instructions to different people at different times based on their current emotions. For example, one time they say, "ask me every time!" and another time we say, "why are you asking me? You should know this!"

This leads to a "he said, she said" situation, which can end up as arguments at best and a valued teammate leaving at worst. ***Key Point:*** Having written processes, policies, and procedures enables team members at all levels of seniority to play by the same rules and have a source of truth to refer to and hold each other accountable to.

What's happening here is a lack of our Super Skill, Connection. What we intended to say may not have been said, or if it was what we intended, they didn't understand it that way. We had bad communication.

Worse yet is verbally giving different instructions and expectations to teammates with the same experience and role. For example, you have two new hires that were hired on different days for your sales team. One you liked a lot, and you were in an especially giving mood when you hired them, so you offered them a higher commission than the other, who you didn't like as much and who was hired on a bad day. What do you think is going to happen when the one with the lower commission finds out? I can assure you that they are going to find out, and it's not going to be pretty. At best, you lose that new hire (there goes another $50k down the toilet). At worst, the one with the higher commission didn't realize you played favorites, and that doesn't align with the Culture you said you had and his core values. You guessed it, another flush down the toilet.

If I can give owners one piece of valuable advice, it's to treat everyone equally and have a consistent way of doing things. We'll get more into this in the chapters on Finance and Accountability. We have to determine what type of organization we will be and how we will communicate our expectations clearly, uniformly throughout our hierarchy, and within our policies and procedures.

Let's start with your Organization. This is different from the environment that you determined in the chapter on Culture. If your Culture is the environment that your team works in, your Organization is how they communicate in that environment. When your Organization is well defined, everyone knows who is in a position of authority and who they are accountable to. When it's not, you'll know it, because you'll see your team circumventing their direct leader whenever they get an answer they don't want; and guess who they will go to next? You guessed it: YOU. It's the old trick we played as kids. If we didn't get what we wanted from Mom, we'd go ask Dad. He always said, "yes."

It is critical that you define and communicate your chain of command and *never* undercut that leader's authority unless it conflicts with your Culture. I really loved it when I was able to ask, "What did your Sales Manager say? Well, they know what they're doing, and they're following our procedures, so I guess that's the way it's gotta be. Now go get it done. I know you can."

Talk about a sense of relief. I trust that my Sales Manager is doing an excellent job, I'm not the bad guy, and I'm the guy earning respect from my team and leaders because they know I trust in them not only in word, but in DEED.

Key Point: When you undercut the authority of one of your leaders, they aren't really the leader anymore—you are. By making an exception, you've told the entire team that exceptions are okay. That mindset will spread like a virus through your whole business. You've literally enabled everyone to break the rules whenever they think it's best, and not just procedurally but also culturally. *Nothing ruins a business faster than "just this one time" decisions.* When we make them, we don't consider the effect they'll have. It's just one tiny decision after all, no big deal.

Every decision we make has a return on investment and leads us down a path. There are two endpoints on that path. Failure (poor ROI) or success (exceptional ROI). While that little decision didn't seem big at the time, it makes it easier and easier for you and the team to make similar decisions that get larger in consequence. "Give 'em an inch, and they'll take a mile," as the old saying goes. Organization is all about Leadership Habit #7, expect. If you don't post anything else on the wall in your office, post that habit. It will remind you that before you make a snap decision that doesn't seem like a big deal, you could be undercutting someone else's authority and responsibility, which causes everyone to lose respect for you as a leader.

In order to eliminate these situations, we need to implement a few things to clearly communicate the expectations of our organization.

Let's get to work...

Step 1: What type of organization are we?
The first thing we need to do is figure out what type of Organization we are and how we will communicate. Are we the one we want to be? Does it fit our Culture and Process? Does it fit the type of leader you are or want to be?

- Are we a Corporate Organization? Do we want to be?
- Are we a Team Organization? Do we want to be?
- Are we a Recruiting/MLM (multi-level marketing) Organization? Do we want to be?
- Are we a Do-Whatever-It-Takes Organization? Do we want to be?
- Are we a Kingdom Organization? Do we want to be?
- Are we a Managing Partner Organization? Do we want to be?
- Are we a Franchise Organization? Do we want to be?
- Are we a Nomadic Warlord Organization? Do we want to be?
- Are we a Mergers and Acquisitions Organization? Do we want to be?

I'm sure there are more organizational types out there, but these are the types we see most often. You may be one of the ones I mentioned but, if not, make sure to define what type of organization you are.

Here's a brief description of each to help you better understand the differences, at least for the ones I mentioned above.

Corporate

This is the most well-known and traditional structure for American business. It incorporates C-Level Executives as they grow an influential Board of Directors. It is usually described as very well organized with procedures strictly enforced. It's driven by data, metrics, and the bottom line. The sales team is normally focused on sales, not lead generation or project management. This may lead to a lower commission percentage but a higher average annual sales revenue. While it's sometimes described as stifling and boring, with the right leadership, a Corporate Organization can be great to work for.

Team

This is structured more like a sports franchise. There's an Owner, General Manager, and various Coaches for sales, administration, and production. Other coaches are added as new Department Leads are needed and as one of the original Coaches cannot wear the hat any longer. For example, the Sales Coach is giving up the responsibility of marketing to a Marketing Coach. Each Coach is solely responsible for their department and held accountable for it by the General Manager, who is often the Owner early in its growth as an Organization. Within each department, additional Coaches may exist as the Organization grows. For example, having multiple Team Leads in a specific department like sales. Each Team Lead manages a small group that is a part of the overall department team. Each Team Lead is held accountable to the results of their specific team. The sales team can be organically grown from recruiting experienced free agents.

Recruiting/MLM

MLM Organizations allow for more autonomy and flexibility than the other Organizations. The MLM Organization is started by the owner, who then recruits others to do what he does, which normally is everything. The new recruit earns a significant commission because they are managing the entire job from start to finish. The deeper the MLM leg goes, the less commission the leader receives at each level. There are usually no quotas or expectations set for MLM Organizations. They follow the "eat what you kill" thought process without much emphasis on training, other than "ride with me and then do what I do." MLM Organizations tend to morph into one of the other Organizations as they grow to provide more structure and support.

Do-Whatever-It-Takes

This is usually a very small Organization made up of family and friends that wear all the hats as needed to get the job done. While it can be profitable and enjoyable to be a small Organization at times, it is impossible to grow without any structure, processes, or system. While sometimes enjoyable, the lack of structure leads to someone feeling that another isn't pulling their weight. This can lead to a constant state of roller coaster results.

Kingdom

There is only one King to rule them all, and they are usually very flamboyant and bordering on arrogant. In the Organization's early years, the King was very charismatic with a vision of domination. As the kingdom grows, Nobles and Lesser Nobles are given dominion over parts of the kingdom—as long as they continue to perform and "pay their taxes." The sales team that performs is treated as royalty. The ones that don't perform are downtrodden until they leave the kingdom. Their lack of performance is usually due more to the leadership than their ability. The Peasants and Serfs are the support team and are rarely recognized for their contributions, causing a lot of turnover. These types of Organizations tend to rise to prominence very quickly but dissolve just as quickly because the King has gotten lazy, and everyone else wants their own throne. It is a rare occasion when the King recognizes the error of his ways early enough to convert his kingdom into a more stable business Organization, but when they do, they usually build amazing companies.

Managing Partner

Managing Partner Organizations are designed around expansion through new locations. The strategy of the Owner is to identify worthy leaders and offer them a "partnership" in a new location. This can take on various forms. Some Managing Partner Organizations offer complete autonomy to operate the location with simply the company name for credibility and little, if any, oversight. Some are little more than sales Organizations with headquarters support for administrative duties. While others are little more than General Managers, who are fully accountable to the company's administration, operations, and sales processes, and who receive some profit sharing based on results. This type of organization can expand rapidly and successfully if they emphasize leadership training. If they aren't successful or experience high turnover, the issue lies usually in proper training, support, and supervision. Many times, Managing Partners feel they aren't getting a big enough slice of the pie for what they're doing and either go off on their own or, worse, start not caring about or reporting results. These types of Organizations tend to have a small group of managing partners carrying the weight for the rest of the Organization. Managing Partner Organizations tend to lack structure across the Organization.

Franchise

A Franchise Organization has created a repeatable process that can be learned by anyone, but it tends to be executed with varying degrees of success. They tend to have more administrative, marketing, and training support than Managing Partnerships, but otherwise are similar in structure. The Franchisee is an Owner of that location unlike the Managing

Partner, but their success or failure is ultimately up to them. Franchisees normally pay a portion of their profits to the Franchisor for administrative and marketing support and a royalty fee for the use of the company name and Process.

Nomadic Warlord

A Nomadic Warlord Organization usually has a charismatic leader like the Kingdom Organization, but they aren't concerned with broad domination. A Nomadic Warlord Organization is usually a small, tight-knit group that goes where opportunity exists in an effort to grab as much of that opportunity as possible. When the opportunity starts to dry up and perceived opportunity looks better elsewhere, they move on. Only the strong survive in the Nomadic Warlord Organization. The weak are left by the wayside as the tribe moves on. Nomadic Warlord Organizations only last for a few years at best, as the thirst for conquest wanes in the Warlord, and the next strongest member of the tribe takes his followers to make a whole new tribe. Like kingdoms, sometimes these Warlords see the writing on the wall and can't keep up that pace forever. They end up settling down in a market that suits them to build a more traditional Organization. These new Organizations—unlike the Kingdom Organizations—tend to be small and profitable enough to enjoy a comfortable lifestyle.

Mergers and Acquisitions

These types of Organizations usually evolve from a long-standing, successful location in a middle to major market that they dominate. They have proven processes and systems and the back office support to expand. Their strategy is to find the right fit for their culture in an established business in another location at the right price. The location can't be so big that the price tag is too high, but they would like it to be an established company with name recognition and a large customer list without refined processes and systems. Boom! Install the processes and system with the headquarters backend support and a strong marketing budget, and you can grow a location with a great name in a hurry.

So what type of Organization are you? What do you want your Organization to be? Are you something completely different? Are you a hybrid of a couple? Are you morphing from one to another? Make sure that whatever type of Organization you are, it aligns with the Culture you've started to instill.

If you don't know what kind of Organization you want to be, you're going to have a hard time figuring out an organizational chart.

Step 2: Accountability Chart
Speaking of organizational charts, that's the next step in *The Contractor's Blueprint* for Organization & Human Resources (but we don't call them organizational charts, and you shouldn't think of them that way). They are *Accountability Charts* for how your team will communicate throughout your Organization.

Now, you may be asking yourself, if this is an "accountability chart," why aren't we discussing that in the chapter on Accountability? As I mentioned in the beginning of this book, each of your Contractor DNA strategies happen in an order. Without creating the accountability chart, at this point we wouldn't have the cornerstone for the work we do in the chapter on Accountability. All that I ask is that you trust me. It'll make perfect sense when you're all done.

You know what time it is? It's time to Write it Down!

Who is at the top of your company? Who's on every level after that? What's the chain of communication and command?

Helpful Hints
- You'll find this task easier if you write it out on paper or a dry erase board first.
- Don't use people's names yet, just their titles. You can put the names in the digital copy that is easier to edit.
- A great tool for your final version is a digital flowchart tool like "Lucidcharts."
- Get your key players involved in helping you with this task.

Step 3: Company Handbook
Now that we know what kind of Organization we are and how authority, information, and communication will flow through that Organization, we need to formalize things a bit more with a company handbook. The idea behind the company handbook is three-fold. First, it is an introduction to your business and a guide to help new team members settle into their new role. Second, it's a clear communication of your policies, procedures, perks, and expectations. Third, it stops more questions, giving you even more capacity! The answers to all those questions are there for all to see in the handbook, and there's no more "he said, she said." If it ain't in the handbook, I didn't say it.

I've done a ton of research, hired consultants, and sought out mentors on developing the perfect handbook. Unfortunately, due to the various organizational types, cultures, procedures, benefits, and job descriptions, there's no one-size-fits-all solution. ***Key Point:*** The best advice I can give you is this: if you're saying anything more than once when it comes to the topics above, get it in your handbook.

In an effort to give you a bit of a head start on creating your company handbook, here's the strategy we use to get started with:

Handbook Purpose
- *Welcome Statement (From the owner)*
- *How to Use This Handbook*
- *Table of Contents*

Company Culture
- *Brief Company Story*
- *Vision Statement*
- *Purpose Statement*
- *Core Values*
- *Accountability Chart*

Employment
- *Employment Classification*
  - *Part Time*
  - *Full Time*
  - *Subcontractor*
- *Any Work Contracts*
- *Working Hours*

Benefits
- *Vacations*
- *Paid Time Off*

- *Healthcare*
- *Retirement*
- *Etc.*

Perks
- *Company Vehicle*
- *Gas Card/Credit Card*
- *Travel Expenses*
- *Company Tools and Equipment*
- *Training and Development*
- *Bonus incentives*

Code of Conduct
- *Protection of Company Property*
- *Diversity and Anti-Harassment*
- *Health and Safety*
- *Social Media*
- *Dress Code*

Processes and Procedures
- *The Ideal Process*
- *Other Processes*
- *Procedures*
  - *Pay Periods or Submissions for Payroll*
  - *Request for Time Off*
  - *Performance Reviews*
  - *Meetings*
  - *Etc.*
- *Recruiting Incentive*
- *Attendance Expectations*

Company Initiatives
- *Community Outreach*
- *Company Charity/Foundation*
- *Recognition Programs*
- *Leadership Programs*

That should give you a pretty good start, and that's the key: just start. Start small with this strategic outline. A lot of what you'll need in your handbook will be created by following *The Contractor's Blueprint*. We've already done the Culture and ideal process, so there's your start. Keep adding to it as you find yourself answering the same questions over and over about policies and procedures.

Helpful Hints
- Don't make this the rulebook. Keep it focused on the positive aspects of working for your business and minimize the negative. No one likes consequences, but we have to set grounds for reprimand and termination. Just don't make a big deal about them; state them factually and move on.
- A really great friend of mine, Matt Grassmyer, introduced me to a book called *The Power of Moments* by Chip and Dan Heath. This book was so good, and I highly suggest you read it. It will change the way you look at the moments in your life and those of others you connect with. It's changed the way we coach. In that book is an amazing statistic. **Key Point:** 90% of all new hires decide on their first day on the job that they're going to quit. Wow! That blew me away when I read it, but it makes sense. It might not be that day, but they know that they're going to eventually quit. They perceive it as just a job—not a career. Your business is not a place they can see themselves working forever. We can bring that percentage down significantly by creating a *Powerful Moment* that very first day. Your handbook should be one of those powerful moments. There are all kinds of opportunities to create powerful moments, so be on the lookout for them.
- Don't make your handbook the encyclopedia of everything. Use the K.I.S.S. Method and Keep It Simple

Stupid. Use the gift of technology to your advantage. For example, don't include 50 pages on your health insurance benefits. Provide a link to the policy in the handbook. That's enough.

- Finally, you may want to consider dedicating one section of your handbook to the job description and expectations section. This way you can switch that section out depending on who you're hiring. It will keep your Handbook smaller and provide everything that a teammate needs all in one place.

This brings us to the final step in the chapter on Organization & Human Resources.

Step 4. Job Descriptions

The great part of *The Contractor's Blueprint* is that by working in order on each of the Contractor DNA strategies, you'll make each of the following strategies easier. You've already done a lot of the heavy lifting here when you created your Process. Remember when we assigned the roles to each step? Well now we know everything that someone in a particular role is responsible for, which is going to make creating your job descriptions drastically easier.

Traditionally, job descriptions have been nothing more than a boring list that includes Job Requirements, Job Duties, and sometimes Job Expectations. If they're *really good*, they include Training Requirements, Benefits, Reporting Authority, and even possibly Compensation. If they're *great*, they start off with a General Description of the job and mention the Culture of the company.

That's most businesses. Sadly, it is rare that we start off with a new coaching client who has actual written job descriptions. I don't know what it is about contractors/

entrepreneurs and investing time up-front to make things easier in the end, but they just don't seem to do it. Maybe they like things the hard way. Come to think of it, a lot of my home services contractor friends on Facebook list their education as "School of Hard Knocks." That explains a lot. Let's see if we can change that to "School of Work Smarter, Not Harder."

While there's nothing necessarily wrong with that job description format above, I wouldn't call it a compelling reason to make that a career—at least when it comes to working in the home services contracting world. I don't think anyone was excited about being an Office Manager, a Production Manager, a Project Coordinator, an Office Admin, a Crew Member or Foreman, or even a Salesperson or Sales Manager for a home services contractor when they were thinking about their dream job.

It's our job to make them see the light and opportunity that is available in the trades. This needs to be their dream job. One of the best places to do this is in your job description. Another opportunity for a powerful moment.

First, let's begin with the format. The one I described earlier isn't terrible, but let's make this compelling.

Instead of naming it a "General Description," which gives a dry 50,000ft view of their job, try "How You Will Impact Our Community." Be sure to include how their role plays a part in making your community a better place. ***Key Point:*** All it takes to create a compelling job description is a little creativity that is in alignment with your awesome Culture, and you can put together one hell of a job description that will have people begging to work for you. Remember though, if you make this sound like the most amazing job on the planet, you had better make sure it is.

Let's get to work…

Step 4.1: Job Description Format
So, let's run down that format again:
- General Description
- Job Requirements
- Job Duties
- Job Expectations
- Training Requirements
- Reporting Authority
- Benefits
- Compensation

Ugggh, I almost fell asleep writing it. Does that sound like an exciting job full of opportunity? If so, run with it. It might just be the ticket if you've chosen a Corporate Organization. For the rest of you, how does this sound?
- How You Will Make An Impact
- Expert Experience
- How You Will Help the Team
- How You Will Feel Challenged
- Get Better Every Day
- Meet Your Mentor/Coach
- How We Care For You
- Reward For a Job Well Done

It's literally the exact same format, but that job sounds way cooler than the first one. Which one would you choose?

Now that you have an example, I challenge you to use your own creativity to develop a format that fits your culture and environment. Remember, your format should be compelling, but also realistic. Don't include any promises or systems you don't currently have in place or will have in place for them. Don't just stick with the example I just gave you. Yeah, it's pretty compelling, but could it be better?

Keep the Organization in mind as you create your job descriptions. If you're a Corporate Organization, make it more corporate. If you're a Team Organization, use sports terminology to explain concepts.

Last but not least—as I mentioned earlier in the book when we were building the process—don't be scared to be creative with the job titles. "Sales Representative" is a bit boring, and it comes with a negative stigma. How about "Home Solutions Expert"?

A final note on this step. If you're having a hard time being creative, you're most likely not the Idealist Leader. If you know one, get their help. If you don't, you need to find one, either from your current team (an opportunity to empower a Job Description Champion) or hire one. They will take your business to heights you never thought possible. If hiring one isn't an option, hire us as your coach. We've got idealism and creativity down to an art form, and you just may learn how you can improve in that aspect as a leader.

Step 4.2: The Description
Much like we did with the format, we have to make the descriptions of each section compelling.

Under Job Requirements/Expert Experience, instead of listing, "Two years Microsoft Excel experience," how about trying, "You're a Spreadsheet Wizard." To ensure that they are a wizard, have them take a test with common expertise you would need from someone working on spreadsheets for you.

Under Job Expectations/How You Will Feel Challenged, instead of putting, "Make 15 sales calls weekly," try, "Give 15 members of our community the opportunity to choose you!" Words are powerful things.

Go through each section of your job description for a particular position, referring back to the Process for duties and experience, and cover everything so the expectations of that particular position are clear and set from day one.

When it comes to Compensation, Benefits, Perks, Non-Competes, or Subcontractor Agreements, include those as addendums to the main job description. These tend to change often enough that they will be easier to edit and update as separate addendums to the original job description.

Some other things you should consider in your job descriptions:
- Compensation in the event of termination or quitting.
- Sign off agreement for use of company equipment and a value if damaged or not returned.
- Signature line for the new teammate and the company representative authorized to hire as a sign of agreement to the job description and any addendums.

If your job description is something you plan to

enforce as a legal document, seek the advice of an attorney, but don't sacrifice culture over attorney advice[1]. One thing about attorneys: they write agreements to ensure that they win in court every time. I want agreements that ensure that we win in business 99% of the time.

I'll never forget having a client skip out on a $65k job. I took them to court and lost because of our contract. I was so mad, and I had an attorney write a lock tight agreement guaranteed to win in court. Our closing percentage was cut in half, costing us $500k over the first 30 days that we started using it, not to mention the attorney fees to write it. That agreement was scary to every customer who read it, and we immediately reverted back to a simpler contract. You don't want your job description to be so intimidating, restricting, and one sided that no one wants to work for you.

Key Point: I promise if you invest the time now to build great job descriptions, the quality of talent that joins your team will improve dramatically.

Now, I know what you're thinking, that's a whole lot of work, and truthfully it is. How do I know that's what you're thinking? We hear it from our clients every day. But we help our clients get through it together by starting with the most important job descriptions first, then the others get done when the need arises. So suck it up and get to work. Build that job description you need now. You have the strategy and the know-how to create the ones you will need in the future.

Once your amazing new job description is built, make sure to

---

1   I am not an attorney and in no way am I supplying you or advising you on how to approach your business from a legal standpoint.

include it in the company handbook when it's given to a new hire.

A final note on job descriptions: just because you have one now doesn't mean it's time to go crazy hiring new teammates. You have more to do with *The Contractor's Blueprint* before you have everything you need to ensure the success of that new hire. Patience now solves huge issues later from hiring a team before you are ready.

With the tools from this chapter you will create an organization that knows how to communicate everything clearly. When we communicate the right way we optimize the experience of the teammates we have creating an environment of high performance. By focusing on our people and their success, they focus on the success of our clients.

"A slack hand causes poverty, but the hand of the diligent makes rich."
—Proverbs 10:4

Chapter 5:
Numbers & Finance

First things first: I am not a CPA. However, I do understand the value of having a great one, and I strongly encourage you to retain a CPA that knows the trades industry. On the other hand, I am a numbers guy, and due to some earlier transgressions in my entrepreneurial journey, I deeply understand the value of knowing my numbers *and* managing my finances.

I know, numbers can be interesting and sometimes even fun, but finance… well that's a whole other story. I promise this will not be a chapter from an accountant's point of view; it will be from a contractor's point of view. It should keep you from making the same mistakes I did by underestimating the value of knowing my numbers and managing my finances.

So what's the difference between "numbers" and "finance"? Well, numbers are the statistical data in various aspects of your business, like percentages of material, labor and overhead relating to the work you do, as well as the top and bottom line numbers like revenue and profit. They also include metrics on sales and efficiency. Finance on the other hand, is the management of the results of those numbers when making decisions on how best to spend or save your money.

See? Numbers are cool! Finance is boring. Not really, though—

they are both cool! Once you understand how they relate to each other and how powerful having a strong understanding of both can play a major factor in the success or failure of your business.

Based on our coaching experience over the last seven years and my 36 years of being an entrepreneur, I feel pretty confident in saying that a lack of knowledge when it comes to your numbers and managing your finances is the second biggest killer of businesses. If you agree with me on that, then it's time to build a strategy for it.

Numbers

We've all been told that we need to know our numbers, but *what* numbers and *why*? When we get to this part with our clients, it is absolutely shocking how many don't know their numbers. Here are the actual stats from our clients through our first seven years and some of the numbers you need to know. These stats are the percentage of home services contractors that ACCURATELY know the following about their numbers before coaching:

- 34.3 % know their Actual Annual Revenue
- 10.7% know their Actual Overhead Expenses
- 13.8% know their Accurate Average Job Revenue
- 7.4% know their Actual Material Percentage of Revenue
- 8.1% know their Actual Labor Percentage of Revenue
- 11% know their Actual Gross Profit
- 1.2% know their Accurate Commissions Percentage of Revenue
- 5.6% know their Actual Net Profit
- <1% know their Accurate Cash Flow (this is the scariest of all the stats)
- <1% know their Actual Revenue by Trade
- <1% know their Actual Costs by Trade

- <1% know their Actual Costs by Individual Material Item
- <1% know their Actual Net Profit by Trade
- 1.7% know their Accurate Annual Budget
- 9.2% know their Actual Closing Percentage
- 2.3% know their Actual Cost Per Lead
- <1% know their Actual Cost Per Acquisition

Now, you may be a numbers type of person and know these numbers about your business. If so, you are to be commended. You are in the elite minority.

On the other hand, you might be like some of our clients that say they know those numbers, but if you look closely at the description of each statistic, you'll notice we use the words "actual" and "accurate" on every single one. ***Key Point:*** The truth is that a lot of us think we know the numbers but really don't. We know when a client uses the word "about" when describing their numbers to us that they are most likely way off and in the favor of "good numbers."

For example, we'll ask if you know your closing percentage, and you'll tell us it's "about 40%." Then we'll take the actual number of contracts and divide that by the number of appointments where a presentation was given, and the number is actually 32%. That is a monstrous 8% difference!

Think about it. If your company runs 100 appointments in a month where a presentation is given, and the average sale is $10k, then you think you're getting 40 new jobs for $400k in revenue at a 40% close rate. In reality, you're getting 32 new jobs for $320k at a 32% close rate. That's an $80,000 difference! I don't know about you, but $80,000 is still a huge number to me! It's not just a lot of money either. It's going to cause a lot of bad financial decisions. And that is just one month! What happens when you compound that mistake over a year? I assure you, nothing good.

When they start with us, the majority of our clients have no clue what their numbers are except for maybe revenue and jobs sold. They just know that they either made money or they didn't, based on what's in their bank account at that particular time. This is no way to operate a business. Is that money in your account really yours or your customers? Have you considered your work in progress, bills to be paid, or commissions you still owe? Are you really making money? Without accurate numbers, who knows? How much more could you have in that bank account if you had a better understanding of your numbers? You'll never know without accurate numbers. The balance in your bank account is not indicative of whether you are making money or not.

When it comes to accuracy, a key point is the distinction between sales and revenue. Revenue is truly owned by production, as it is driven by the completion of jobs. Marketing fills the sales pipeline and sales fills the production/revenue pipeline, which is what drives your P&L, or true accurate profitability. When you look at your numbers in those three buckets—marketing, sales, and production—you start to see where your bottlenecks are. If your production team can't keep up with your sales numbers (meaning your revenue each month is consistently less than your sales), you know you have a bottleneck in your production team. Many contractors get themselves in trouble because they consider the sales as revenue. However, you have a whole lot of overhead to earn that money, and if production can't complete the work, then you quite simply have not *earned* that money.

Why is accuracy so important? Well, it's a long list:
- You can coach better if you know your Closing Percentage.
- You can buy better if you know your Material Costs and Percentages.

- You can make better decisions in marketing if you know your Lead Cost.
- You can forecast accurately if you know your Revenue Per Job Average, Number of Leads, and Closing Percentage.
- You can make better hiring decisions if you know your Overhead Percentage.
- You can cut or add fixed costs if you know your Overhead Percentage and have Accurate Profit Forecasts.
- You may or may not be able to buy that new truck if you know your actual Cash Flow situation.
- You may or may not be able to take on that huge project if you know your actual Cash Flow situation.

Should you keep doing that type of work or not? You'll never know without knowing your numbers by trade.

Once you get an accurate picture of your numbers, the list of great decisions you can make goes on and on. You can create budgets for various departments and projects to grow your business, get that bigger office, give out bonuses, take a vacation, set aside money for retirement, or give to charity without fear of hurting your business. When you know your numbers, your decisions are made with confidence, not guesses and fear. I promise you will sleep a lot better.

You'd be shocked at how many contractors find out that they're barely breaking even or even losing money on a trade and don't realize it because it's wrapped up in a multi-trade project. We've helped a lot of contractors either charge appropriately or stop doing work they should not be doing. Only later do they realize that they have more time to focus on what they do make money at. Boom! Instantly more profitable!

I hope at this point you're starting to see the value of knowing your numbers and the power that information will afford you when making financial and personnel decisions for your business.

Now, a bit of caution here: don't get so caught up in the numbers that it's all you're doing, and it's the only thing you're basing your decisions on. There is still room for calculated risk and educated instinct. ***Key Point:*** There's a big difference between the numbers you want to know and the numbers you need to know. The larger you grow, the more time you will have to dedicate to all of your numbers. But remember, we are trying to create capacity here, not extra work.

Here's our list of what you accurately need to know at a minimum:

Business Specific Numbers
- Profit & Loss
- Balance Sheet
- Work in Progress (WIP—an accounting term for your paid costs on jobs that are in production)
- Cash Flow
- Revenue by Year, Quarter, and Month
- Overhead

Job Specific Numbers
- Average Revenue per Job and Trade if you do multiple Trades on a Job
- Average Percentage and Cost for Material and Labor per Job and Trade
- Miscellaneous Costs per Job and Trade (i.e., Permits, Dumpsters, etc.)
- Total Percentage of Cost of Goods Sold (COGS) per Job and Trade
- Average Commissions Per Job and Trade (including any bonuses or commissions paid to a manager(s))
- Average Gross Profit Percentage by Job and Trade
- Average Percentage of Gross Profit Compared to Revenue

over the same time period
- Percentage of Overhead as it relates to Revenue for the same time period
- Average Percentage of Net Profit Compared to Revenue over the same time period

Sales Specific Numbers
- Sales Revenue by Team for Year, Quarter, Month and Week
- Sales by Rep for Year, Quarter, Month, and Week
- Total Sales Pipeline
- Average Time to Close
- Closing Percentage by Team and Rep
- Activity Key Performance Indicators (KPI's) by Team and Rep (we'll cover this in more detail in the chapter on Accountability)

Marketing Specific Numbers
- ROI per Lead Source
- Number of Leads for a Year, Quarter, Month, and Week
- Cost per Lead
- Cost per Acquisition

Now, some of you just read all that, your brain turned to Jell-O, and now you're trembling in the corner. Others of you are chomping at the bit and want more. Still, others are saying, "I don't have time for all this, we've got sales to make and jobs to do. I know my numbers well enough."

For those of you trembling in the corner, get some help with this. Everything I listed comes down to a pretty simple math equation that you can Google or have a bookkeeper or CPA help you with. You could also hook up with one of our coaches and we can guide you through it. We dig numbers! Remember to start small. Get an accurate revenue and average job, then start to work on costs, then overhead. Before you know it, you'll have an accurate gross and net profit. With just that limited information, you'll be able to make smarter decisions financially.

For those of you chomping at the bit with numbers, metrics, and beautiful charts and graphs dancing through your head: slow down. Start small, get these preliminary tasks done and then add to it with the numbers you want to know over time. Remember the old saying, "they can't see the forest for the trees"? This is what can happen if you get too tied up chasing down every number for your business. You will not see the big picture because of the desire to save a penny. We see it all the time with clients who know they can save money buying in bulk. They certainly can, but if they don't have the systems to keep proper inventory to ensure that materials don't "grow legs" and walk off and a process to get the materials to the site, they end up spending more time getting deliveries done. Both of which eat up all the savings that they thought they would have, and in the end it will cost more than just having the material delivered by a supplier. I am by no means saying it can't be done, but you need to do it right to realize the savings.

For those of you that "know your numbers well enough," I can assure you that you don't. I'm speaking from experience here—I was one of you. I had the advantage of being able to see math in my head better than anyone I knew, and I still made massive financial mistakes that almost put me out of business more than once. There's another problem with this approach: your ability to grow and scale your business is severely hampered because you keep making bad financial decisions. Additionally, even if you are good at it, you're the only one that sees what you see, so there is no help to be had from those with better financial management skills.

I have vendors and suppliers tell me all the time that the contractors they work with seem financially strong from the outside because their sales are strong, they drive big trucks, and have an awesome office, but they aren't paying their bills on time or at all. Their turnover is high because they aren't paying their team on time. All because they don't know their numbers and how to manage their finances.

Step 1: Know Your Numbers

Using the list of needed numbers above, pick an appropriate time frame or number of jobs that gives you a fairly accurate number to start with. For example, you can use revenue going back a year for an accurate sample size. For the numbers related to jobs and trades, go back 30-50 jobs, and you'll get pretty close. As you start to track from this point forward, the numbers will get more and more accurate until they are exact.

For those of you with accounting software like QuickBooks, you should get some of the data you need, but if you have to go file by file to get it figured out, you need to do so. Yes, it is a painful process but worth it to get accurate numbers. You will also see the value in having a system that will get you these numbers at any point in time. It will be easier to maintain once you start using your financial software and CRM data to generate your numbers at any time. That information can be exported into some pretty amazing spreadsheet reports to track them and use as a dashboard to make great decisions.

What about those of you that just don't have any accurate historical information or financial software? First off, get QuickBooks. It is the most standardized accounting software out there. It is fairly simple to learn the basics, and almost any decent bookkeeper or accountant will be familiar with it. A bit of caution here when it comes to outsourced bookkeepers and accountants. Our industry has specific and unique needs that require a process to determine accurate numbers. The companies we see with the greatest success in this category have a Finance Champion, and they get them the right training. Finally, start tracking today—even if you have to write it down—and within 30-90 days you're going to have pretty accurate numbers, and you'll start making better decisions.

Earlier, I gave you some resources for the equations you'll need to figure out your numbers, but maybe you just aren't an accounting software or spreadsheet type just yet (you will need to learn). If you want to make this a lot easier, you can do a quick Google search for the spreadsheets I mentioned or ask your bookkeeper or CPA for help. After all, it is what you pay them for.

If that still isn't enough, set up a free strategy call with us here at Contractor Coach PRO, and we'll give you a hand.

Step 2: Budgeting - The Profit Pie™
Now that you know your numbers, you can start budgeting for expenses. You can now forecast revenue, costs, and profit based on accurate data and presumed sales. Think of the revenue that you generate as your favorite pie. The problem is that there is only so much of that pie to go around.

This brings us to the Profit Pie™. We have to understand what money is available and how much we should be allocating for things like commissions, bonuses, manager pay, and marketing. First, you need to understand what percentages you currently pay. Then, you'll need to allocate the right amount for where we want to be in the future. Make sure you consider expenses like new hires and marketing as well as non-overhead percentages like sales manager or team leader commissions.

The best way to visualize this is as a pie chart that is based on your average job. There's only 100% of that job to go around, and I'm assuming you would like some of it in the end.

Let's do an example. We'll use a $10,000 job to make the math easier to understand:

For a $10,000 job:
- *Revenue: $10,000*
- *Material: $3000 / 30%*
- *Labor: $2500 / 25%*
- *Permit: $100 / 1%*
- *Dumpster: $400 / 4%*
- *Commissions: $1000 / 10%**
- *Gross Profit: $3000 / 30%*

*Based on our experience, we strongly recommend that you pay your commissions as a percentage of revenue for reasons that we will cover in the next chapter. But if you pay off the gross profit, flip the order of the last two rows and add another row at the bottom for "Adjusted Gross Profit."

Note: For those of you that include some fictitious (yes, it's fictitious!) number for "overhead" as a job cost, please, for the love of God—STOP! All this does is open an opportunity for disagreement with your sales team on the accuracy of that number and whether you are truly providing for your actual overhead or skimming off the revenue of the job to line your pockets. It also precludes you from accurately determining your numbers from an accounting perspective. On the other hand, if you want to include a fee or percentage of the job as an "admin" or "support" cost, more power to you. Just stop calling it "overhead." Be clear and transparent.

At this point, you should have a number for either Gross Profit or Adjusted Gross Profit. That's the number that everything else comes out of. Indirect Costs like third party services that are not directly related to the job (canvassers and telemarketing might be an example of this, as they are paid by the lead but not necessarily part of your overhead), management cost allocation, and overhead.

Let's say you want to hire a sales manager. You're tired of working 80 hours a week, and you need more time to work on your business. How much are you willing to allow in your budget per job for that position?

In the example above, we have $3,000 left over. If your accurate overhead is 15%, that leaves us with $1,500 in net profit (i.e., your piece of the pie). How much of that are you willing to give up to budget for a sales manager? Let's say you decide to budget 5% and assume that, along with running everything, you've been able to manage 100 jobs. You figure that a good sales manager should be able to manage 75 jobs (they aren't you after all) and hire three more sales reps under them that can also do 75 jobs. That would be a total of 300 instead of 100 jobs, and they'd likely be better managed. You're also definitely less stressed.

Let's do the numbers...

If we allocate 5% to the manager budget, and we do 300 jobs at $10,000, that would be $3 million in revenue generating a budget of $150,000. Is that enough? Too much? Only you can decide that, but our rule of thumb is to budget about $100,000 per $5 million in sales. Remember it's a budget—you don't have to pay the entire amount. Could you instead split it and hire both a sales manager and production manager? There's another hat off your head, and you're still ending up with 10% or $300k instead of the $150k you were making doing it yourself. If your managers are really good and your Finance Champion is great, could they spend more time making the jobs more profitable? Maybe they could increase your 10% cut up to 12%, 13% or even back up to the original 15% or more? Mine were able to, and yours will be too because they're totally focused on one job while you were focused on many. With all that spare time and extra money, could you put that into more marketing so your sales manager could hire more reps and do even more jobs? Put it in the Profit Pie™ and see if it's in the budget[1].

You can see a sample of the Profit Pie™ in Figure 5.1 on the next page.

Finance

Finance is all about taking all of your accurate numbers and managing your money based on past, current, and forecasted data compared to your budgets. For example, can we buy that new truck? I'm not sure. Let's take a look at the cash flow and overhead reports to see if it works in the budget. Some of you are going to hate this level of accountability to numbers— it's your money after all, and you're used to buying what you need/want whenever it suits your fancy. I promise you'll love me for it when you know you can buy that truck, still get your bills paid, and achieve your Dream! Don't forget about The Dream—it's what all this effort is for!

Now, it's been our experience that the vast majority of contractors are not very good accountants, CPA's, or bookkeepers,

---

1   You can download the Profit Pie™ worksheet at https://bit.ly/profitpie.

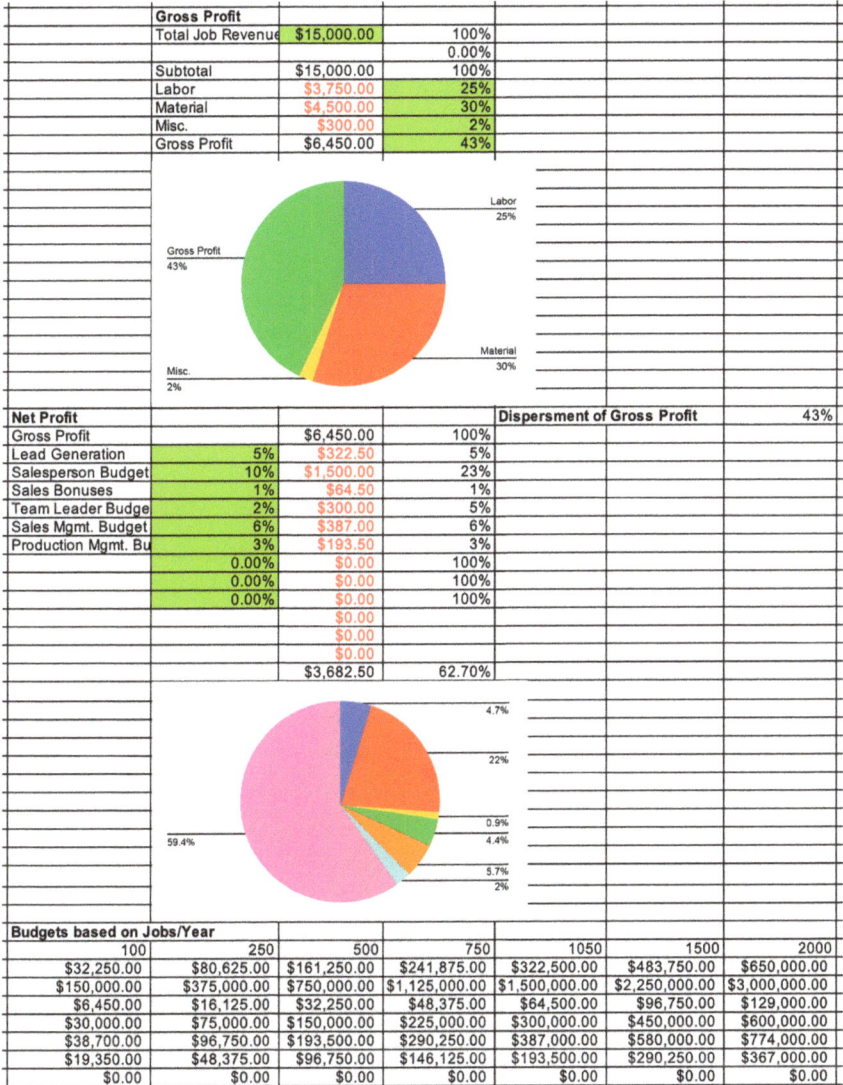

	Gross Profit					
	Total Job Revenue	$15,000.00	100%			
			0.00%			
	Subtotal	$15,000.00	100%			
	Labor	$3,750.00	25%			
	Material	$4,500.00	30%			
	Misc.	$300.00	2%			
	Gross Profit	$6,450.00	43%			

Net Profit				Dispersment of Gross Profit		43%
Gross Profit		$6,450.00	100%			
Lead Generation	5%	$322.50	5%			
Salesperson Budget	10%	$1,500.00	23%			
Sales Bonuses	1%	$64.50	1%			
Team Leader Budget	2%	$300.00	5%			
Sales Mgmt. Budget	6%	$387.00	6%			
Production Mgmt. Bu	3%	$193.50	3%			
	0.00%	$0.00	100%			
	0.00%	$0.00	100%			
	0.00%	$0.00	100%			
		$0.00				
		$0.00				
		$0.00				
		$3,682.50	62.70%			

Budgets based on Jobs/Year						
100	250	500	750	1050	1500	2000
$32,250.00	$80,625.00	$161,250.00	$241,875.00	$322,500.00	$483,750.00	$650,000.00
$150,000.00	$375,000.00	$750,000.00	$1,125,000.00	$1,500,000.00	$2,250,000.00	$3,000,000.00
$6,450.00	$16,125.00	$32,250.00	$48,375.00	$64,500.00	$96,750.00	$129,000.00
$30,000.00	$75,000.00	$150,000.00	$225,000.00	$300,000.00	$450,000.00	$600,000.00
$38,700.00	$96,750.00	$193,500.00	$290,250.00	$387,000.00	$580,000.00	$774,000.00
$19,350.00	$48,375.00	$96,750.00	$146,125.00	$193,500.00	$290,250.00	$367,000.00
$0.00	$0.00	$0.00	$0.00	$0.00	$0.00	$0.00

Figure 5.1

and they really dislike the details of managing their finances.

You should get someone else to do anything you dislike doing as soon as possible. You need a Finance Champion! Those of you that run a smaller business may still be doing this yourself. Those of you that are larger may already have someone in place, but are they a Champion?

For those of you still doing it yourself, how many more jobs could you sell, how many new reps could you hire and train, and how many more referrals and reviews could you get if you had someone taking that burden off of you? All of these are things you hopefully enjoy and drive revenue, which gives you the capital to grow and scale.

There are all kinds of ways to get the help you need. If it's in the budget, hire a bookkeeper and retain a CPA. If that doesn't fit, there are all kinds of third-party virtual accounting and Chief Financial Officer (CFO) companies out there that are far more financially responsible. As a matter of fact, our Financial Coach (and absolute rockstar) offers these types of services to our clients. Remember that Finance Champion we mentioned earlier and getting them the training that they need? Our Finance Coach does that too. Whether you use us or someone else, make sure that they understand finance when it comes to contracting first and foremost!

For those of you that are larger and already have someone on staff, the question you should be asking yourself is this: "Are they a Finance Champion helping us make great, financially responsible decisions, or are they just a bookkeeper?" If it's the latter, it's time to start looking for that CFO, whether virtually or on staff. They are worth their weight in gold and will free you up to do what you do best which is to drive growth.

Step 3: Finance Champion

This is the shortest step I'll probably write in this entire book.

You either need to become the Finance Champion for your business or find one you can trust that has experience working with contractors.

Make sure you sit down with your Finance Champion once a month (at a minimum) to reconcile your accounts. Don't just peruse the high-level P&L, balance sheet, and numbers reports you've created. Dig into the various accounts to make sure that each account balances out with the work you've done for that time period. Keep a sharp eye out for strange items, two payments to the same entity, or amounts that just don't "seem" right. Question them with your Champion. 99% of the time, it's something simple. The other 1%? Well money—or more accurately, greed—can make a good person make bad decisions. You reconciling your accounts ensures that doesn't happen. And if it does happen, you can catch it quickly enough that it's not a huge financial issue.

I find that numbers are the best way to allow owners and leaders to see results of the work their team does, addressing issues as needed instead of micromanaging how someone gets their job done. As long as you have good numbers, the numbers don't lie. It gives you an opportunity to empower your team to think strategically for you. When a budget is set, your numbers can alert you to issues, whether from entry errors or mis-spending. Both are valuable to catch in a timely manner. Trust but verify!

Step 4: Taxes

We have all heard the old saying, "there are only two things you can count on: death and taxes." If we know we have to pay taxes, we should approach it with the best possible strategy. My advice is to consider a Certified Tax Planner (CTP) that you can verify through their clients that they know what they are doing. I wish I would have retained someone sooner! This is another asset to your team that is worth their weight in gold—unless you love paying taxes. These are the people that know how to organize your business from a legal standpoint to optimize your tax savings from S-Corps to C-Corps, LLC's, LLP's, LLP's filing as a C-Corp, Holding Companies to protect your assets, and Foundations to serve your community and save on taxes. I won't pretend to know which is right for your business, but we do know people that do. If you're in need, say so in the "Contractor Community | Control, Growth and Freedom for Contractors" Facebook group, and we'll introduce you. The same goes for CPA's and pretty much any other asset or vendor you need. We've vetted them, and they can be trusted to serve you.

A Cautionary Tale...
If you remember back earlier in the book, I shared about a bookkeeper/minority partner that had embezzled over $500k from our business. Well, in that instance I made one major mistake. I didn't inspect what I expected.

Yes, they stole money—and that was wrong—but it wasn't completely their fault. Yep, here I am again asking myself "why?" Why on earth would they do this? Well, a lot of it came down to the fact that my other partner and I trusted them way too much. We own much of the blame. You see, in this person's opinion, they should have been an equal partner but was not. We explained the investment they would need to make at that point in time to be an equal partner, and that just didn't sit right with them, so they continued with their percentage of ownership. Little did we realize how determined they were to be an equal partner, so they simply started taking what they thought was rightfully theirs.

My partner and I never really looked at the books other than the high-level P&L and balance sheet statements because we all *trusted* each other.

I can remember the day I learned the hard lesson of "trust but verify." It was the middle of January in Minnesota. The only people in the office were me and my other partner, who led the production side of our business. The mail showed up, which we never went through because we had people for that. But that day we did. Sure enough, there was a bank statement in it. A big, thick envelope with the statement and dozens of cancelled checks. My partner and I had never opened one, ever! That day we did…

Suffice it to say, it was like opening Pandora's Box. There were all kinds of checks for things that didn't make sense. Checks to their spouse—who happened to work for us— but they weren't payroll checks. A check for an air conditioner in Chicago. We didn't do A/C work, and we didn't have an office in Chicago (yet). It was at that point that we opened up QuickBooks and started to look deeper than the P&L. There were all kinds of discrepancies throughout various accounts. My partner was like a bloodhound, and over the next two weeks they were able to verify $500k+ that was missing! I was devastated, and he was pissed. We were mad at the employee and mad at each other. The reality is that we should have been mad at ourselves.

I'll end the story there, but I'm sure you can surmise that it went downhill from there. This was absolutely one of the darkest times in my life, all because I trusted too much and because I was more concerned with "me" than "we."

It still hurts to this day, 16 years later. I had failed not only myself, but my family, partners, and team.

I share this story in hopes that you learn from it. If we had just sat down once a month and reconciled the accounts, how different would things be today?

Know your numbers, manage your finances, and trust but verify…

"For which of you, desiring to build a tower, does not first sit down and count the cost, whether he has enough to complete it?"
—Luke 14:28

Chapter 6:
Accountability

Accountability is where the rubber meets the road. If there's a secret ingredient to growth, it's accountability. Accountability is recognizing a standard and being willing to be accountable to that standard.

Accountability is why I knew I was going to destroy the competition as a home services contractor. Remember, back in those days I was all about winning at all costs (I'm not any less about winning today, it's just that winning looks different now. It's more about you than me), and I noticed something right away when I got hired as a sales rep by a home services contractor. Accountability was literally nonexistent!

How much am I supposed to sell? *As much as you can!* When should I follow-up with clients? *When you can fit it in or when they call you.* How many leads should we generate? *As many as possible!* What should a customer expect when we do the job? *A good one!* What should my closing percentage be? *100%!* (well, that's a standard but not too realistic.) What are my hours? *As often as you can.*

I was shocked. I had the freedom to do it any way I wanted. For a highly motivated and disciplined person like myself, this was a relief. First off, some manager wasn't going to be breathing down my neck and upping the bar on me every time I broke a record. Second, I knew I was going to be at the top of sales immediately.

There was something I knew that they didn't: I had a life before contracting. I was a highly trained sales professional, I had managed several hundred salespeople with pretty incredible results (if I do say so myself), and I knew how to be disciplined and hold myself accountable.

If you've done any hiring in this industry, you probably realize how rare of a person that is. We call them "purple unicorns" here at Contractor Coach PRO.

All I had to do was learn the sales process, perfect it, and then look out world—Jim Johnson is gonna run all over you! Only one problem… there was no real sales Process either.

Thankfully, all of those years of both giving and receiving sales training as well as the hundreds of hours spent in leadership training had positioned me to know how to create my own sales Process. We'll get more into that in the chapter on Sales Strategy in my second book.

It took a day or two, but I worked out a process, set some goals, practiced like a maniac, and proceeded to the top of the sales leaderboard within two weeks. I sold more than double of the next guy on the board over the next three months and was promoted to Sales Manager. With the help of an amazing Production Manager and some key support staff, we took a company from selling 400 jobs one year to 4,000 the next!

This is what happens when you marry skill and accountability with a great Process and team.

The challenge most of us face is that there aren't a whole lot of purple unicorns running around out there.

Human behavior studies have proven time and again that without having standards and holding people accountable to them, people will do the minimum of what they *need* to do to get by.

It's truly incredible what happens when you apply standards and then hold people accountable to those standards.

There were literally dozens of other reps hired at the same time as me. Only a select few had success. Mostly because something was personally driving them, and the others… well, they did what they needed to do to get by.

At the time, I just figured it was an anomaly, but years later when I was Director of Sales for the software company I mentioned earlier, I found out that 95% of home services contractors were like that. I was blown away. Why wouldn't you set standards and expectations and hold people accountable to them? You'd be so much more profitable, and your people would be happier. You could identify the companies that had set standards; they were the biggest ones, and depending on what they were accountable to, they were often the best contractors in the market. They knew the trick.

Do you want to hear a really cool statistic? One that proves accountability works? ***Key Point:*** Those 95% of contractors who had no accountability—no matter where they were located, their salespeople averaged $500k per year. Isn't that crazy? We all know the same thing is more expensive the further north, and even more so further northeast. The same goes for the West Coast; things are just more expensive there. Wouldn't it make sense then in California, the Upper Midwest, and the Northeast that a sales reps' annual average sales would be higher? They aren't.

As you probably know by now, I'm a Process guy. Part of my Process is that every time I would go to a new contractor to talk about our software, I would ask what their annual revenue was and how many reps they had. The company would almost always average $500k per rep. At first, I was asking for personal sales reasons. Those two questions let me know if you could afford it and how many users you would have, which in turn determined the sale value when you purchased our software.

It didn't take long for it to become a puzzle that I needed to figure out. I engaged with statistics and economics professors at more than one university, and none of them had an answer until one day one of the economic professors said I should show my findings to someone in Human Behavior. The first question he asked was, "How much should they sell?" It hit me like a ton of bricks! I literally blurted out, "There is no standard! I'm such an idiot. Thank you for your time, and I'm sorry I bothered you." He asked if I wanted to know why it was $500k, and I hadn't really thought about that. I knew I could move the needle with standards and accountability, so it wasn't really all that important to what I needed to know. The reps at my contracting business had averaged a hair over $800k, after all.

I do love to learn though, so I stayed to learn "why" from the professor. The conversation went something like this…

"Sure, I was kind of wondering why it had settled there," I said.

"Well, how much of that do they make?" asked the Professor. "Wait, let me guess, 10-15%?"

"Wow, that's incredible! How'd you know?" I asked.

"Well, the median livable wage in America is $50-$65k, so it comes down to natural human behavior. *Key Point:* They're working as hard as they have to—enough to make a living—because no one is asking them to do more. I bet if you look closer, you will see some slight variance in places that have a higher cost of living, but it won't deviate much," explained the Professor.

Sure enough, he was right. There was a slight variance in places where the cost of living was higher, but not significantly enough that there was a drastic difference.

Man, talk about an epiphany! It was something I also couldn't understand. Why would anyone just want to "make a living"?

That was the day I knew the reason behind my standards. It wasn't about me and my goals—it was about theirs. So many things became clear that day: we need to hire people who are hungry for more than just making a living; we need to understand why they want more, to hold them accountable to it; and it's not necessarily about money or goals, it's about achieving dreams.

Standards challenge people and help them realize their potential. If we don't set them and hold people accountable to them, we're letting them down! *Key Point:* Think about the best you've ever done. I guarantee it was when you were challenged to achieve something, and everyone knew it.

This book is a great example. I've been working on it for three and a half years without a whole lot of progress. I shot a video, posted it online, and told the world it would be done (at least the first draft) in two weeks. Now that's accountability, and there's no way I'm not going to get it done. As of this moment, if I finish this chapter today, I'm right on schedule with that draft.

So, what makes up accountability?
- Minimum Standards (Quota for Sales), Expectations, and Goals
- Clear communication of the Standards
- Agreement that the Standards are achievable and that there are actions and/or consequences when they aren't met
- Reviews to measure results
- Belief in and strict adherence to the Standards

Now, setting standards and holding people accountable to them can be done in a couple of ways. The first is the most common. The standards are set by the company and applied across the board to all team members of equal experience. This approach often involves moving the bar of those expectations once they are met, especially for sales teams. The only problem with this approach is that these standards are more about the company than the individual. The second isn't done nearly as often because it takes a bit more work. It involves sitting down with each individual on the team, investing time to understand their hopes and dreams, and then helping them develop the standards to achieve them. The surprising thing about this approach is that individuals, for the most part, will set their standards beyond what the company would have.

What should we set standards for? EVERYTHING! We've already set standards here in *The Contractor's Blueprint*:
- How we will lead with our 7 Leadership Habits
- The Dream, The Vision, and The Mission to achieve
- The Purpose to follow with passion
- How we will behave with our Core Values
- What type of environment and employee experience we will have
- What type of Organization we will be
- How we communicate in that Organization

- The ideal process we will follow
- The numbers we need to know
- How we will manage our finances

This entire book is about setting standards!

I told you it would become clearer in this chapter why there were accountability items in other chapters. *The Contractors Blueprint* is all about accountability. As a matter of fact, accountability is the real value of our coaching. These are all things you know you should have done long ago. We hold you accountable to get them done. By doing so, you learn how to hold your own team and yourself accountable. ***Key Point:*** When you learn accountability and apply it with great leadership, the possibilities are endless.

So back to the question at hand: what should we set standards for? I think I could write an entire book on just accountability. The problem is, I don't know if anyone would ever read it, and it's not the intention of this book. The purpose of this book is to give you the strategies you need—in the proper order!—to grow and scale your business far beyond where you are today. So let's stick with the basics, and once you get the concept, then you can use the power of accountability to set standards in any areas you want to challenge people to reach their full potential, whether as individuals or as a team.

Let's hit the big ones in sales, as those will be the standards that drive growth immediately. Here are our top three:
1. Production (how much should we sell?)
2. Commissions & Bonuses
3. Activity (how much of what should we be doing?)

Step 1: Production
When it comes to sales, production is how much we want

someone to sell in a given period of time. It is likely that the period of time may be different for different types of contractors and customers. For example, a home security contractor may want a daily standard, while a pool contractor may set a standard per month that varies based on seasonality. Just remember, this book is designed to give you the blueprint. You will need to pick out the "paint colors and flooring" for your particular situation.

To keep continuity, let's use that same $10,000 job that we used before and set up some standards to beat those $500k sales averages for a year with standards set for a week, month, quarter and year. Another thing to keep in mind is that a new recruit has no idea about that $500k average. The only thing they have to go off of is *your standards*. Their assumption is that any standards you set are possible. With our clients, we use the accountability concepts of *Quota, Expected,* and *Goal* to set the standards for production by their sales teams.

Quota, for a lack of a better term, is the minimum standard—the number you have to achieve to stay on the team. If you can't do at least this, the reality is that you're not cut out to be on our team. One of the ways we try to explain this to our clients is by asking this: at what level of production would someone be able to "make a living," and you wouldn't fire them for doing so?

Expected is the amount you're expected to sell in a particular time period.

Finally, the goal is the amount we'd love to see you sell—if you're setting standards as a company. If you are setting standards with each individual, these would be the numbers they would need to produce to achieve their

Dream. Pay particular attention here to the words I am using. If it is company focused, it is about the goal. If it is about the individual, it's about their Dream.

Quota is everything up to expected, and expected is everything over that number up to goal.

The period of time is the cutoff point to determine if you're achieving production standards or not, and if you are achieving those standards, how you'll be rewarded. We'll get to the reward in the next step for commissions and bonuses. Here we're solely concerned with sales production.

To keep it simple, let's set our period of time as a month and play it out over a year with a situation that doesn't have a seasonal difference. If you operate in a seasonal industry or your climate determines seasonality, you would have a bell-shaped set of standards based on that seasonality.

Remember, we want to beat that crappy national average, so let's set it up by starting with the total amount to sell in a year:

Quota: $600k
Expected: $900k
Goal: $1.2 Million

First off, it's not required to be the same difference from one level to the next, but it is highly recommended. Otherwise, your team will start to feel that you're setting goals out of reach so you don't have to pay the extra commission—or that you're simply an unfair ass.

Now let's figure out the monthly standard. Simply divide each number by 12. That would set the monthly standards as follows:

> *Quota: $50k*
> *Expected: $75k*
> *Goal: $100k*

With standards like these, we can easily convert those into a number of jobs someone needs to sell. In this particular example, that would be:

> *Quota: Approximately 5 jobs per month*
> *Expected: Approximately 7.5 jobs per month*
> *Goal: Approximately 10 jobs per month*

At this point, I want to mention that there are simplified versions of this out there called a "quota and over quota system." This is a make-it-or-not approach. By having a three-tiered approach and using words like, "expected" and "goal," people will tend to push a little harder. You'll also find that your average across a team will be higher—usually really close to the expected number on average per rep. Remember, words are powerful things, and most people want to do what is expected at a minimum. No one wants to be in that quota group, especially when we add the jet fuel of incentive in Step 2.

Step 2: Determining Commissions for Sales Accountability*
Now that we know what our standards are for production, we can determine what reward (commissions and bonuses) one can expect for their performance.

There are three things we have to understand about commissions:
1. With more responsibility comes more reward. In other words, the more a rep is responsible for, the

more commissions they should earn. Likewise, the less they're responsible for, the less commissions they should earn. If you think about it, it makes more sense than just what you see on the surface; less for less and more for more. The reality is that both reps will likely end up making approximately the same. The one with a lower commission rate will have more time to make more sales than the one with more responsibility. The sales rep with fewer responsibilities is also easier to train, and typically far happier to do what they do best—which is selling. The sales rep with more responsibilities is likely generating leads, selling, project managing, and collecting payments. This deserves more of the pie because others aren't being compensated for those responsibilities.

2. If the rep is fully responsible for the profitability of the job, then in most cases they should be paid off the gross profit of the job. If the pricing is more controlled, set, or determined by the company or a member of the team other than the sales rep, they should be paid off the revenue.**

3. While standards are important for driving sales, incentive is just as—if not more—important. When we can combine the two, we add jet fuel to our sales team.

*We are only discussing commissions and how they provide for accountability and incentive in this section. Many of our clients have a salary + commission structure to incentivize their team and allow for higher retention of that team. Many of your decisions here were determined earlier in the chapter on Numbers & Finance by using the Profit Pie™ to determine budgets for things like compensation. Remember, the total percentage of that pie that you are willing to pay can be straight commission or a salary + commission structure. The most important aspects of this strategy that you need to understand are that your compensation has to fit within that budget based on the average productivity of your sales team and that there must be incentive to push productivity.

**There is so much that goes into determining whether a rep is paid their commission off of revenue, gross profit, or even recurring revenue. In many cases, it is impossible to include everything in this book. It is one of the reasons why every chapter in this book and one-on-one coaching for your compensation strategy are so important. With all of the different types of contractors, industry products, and underlying belief systems, there is no "silver bullet" solution to commissions when it gets to the specifics of your system. There are, however, best practices of the strategy for commissions. By following the basic strategies above, you should be in a good situation to succeed with your compensation. If you are still having a hard time with compensation after reading this section on commissions, take our free Contractor Assessment to give us a better idea of your strengths and weaknesses. Upon completion of the assessment, you will be emailed a link to our coaching calendar to meet for a free, one-time coaching session with one of our elite coaches. Pick a time that works in your schedule and get an idea of what coaching looks like in an area where you need help[1].

Now that we understand commissions a little better, let's talk about the reward. In order to get any reward, there must be incentive. Without incentive to achieve more, we will revert back to the basic human instinct of survival. A simple example is if we just kept it at quota, expectation, and goal. For a time, the wording of those standards would

---

1   Take the Contractor Assessment at https://s.surveyanyplace.com/ccpassessment

provide a little incentive to at least achieve expectations. Without the additional incentive of improved reward, your team will quickly lose interest. Why would someone push any harder if the reward didn't really change?

For example, if you were to pay a set commission of 10% of the revenue for commissions, what incentive would cause me to push to achieve expectations or a goal other than status or my survival needs? How would that change their productivity if instead, upon achieving the monthly quota we set above in our productivity sample, then someone would earn a commission of 8%, and if they achieved expectations they would get a 2% bonus above the 8% commission, and if they really pushed and hit our goal, they would receive another 2% bonus for a total reward that is 4% more.

Using our productivity standards example above, put yourself in the shoes of a sales rep. It is the third week of June, and up to this point you have sold $56,500 in sales for the month. Whew! You get to stay on the team! Now using the incentive-based commission strategy above, at this point you would have earned $4,520, or 8% of your sales. Using the average sale of $10,000 from our ficti-tious company, you only need to sell two more jobs in the next week to surpass the $75,000 mark to reach expecta-tions and receive a 2% bonus on all of your sales for that month. Would that make a difference in you following up with your sales pipeline? Would that make you call that referral you just got? Would that cause you to knock on another door or make another cold call? If you aren't sure, let's do the math and figure it out.

If you made just two more sales at the average before the end of the month, your total would be $75,500. Boom!

You did what was expected! 8% of that is $6,040—a pretty good incentive. But if there weren't the incentive of a 2% bonus in a limited amount of time, you could have made those sales at any point and still earned the same amount of money, so there is no sense of urgency and thus no additional incentive other than status. If status isn't a driving force for you, human behavior will be your incentive. With the time and the bonus factored in, how does that affect the incentive? Let's do the math.

A 2% bonus on achieving expectations would net us an additional $1,510 on that same $75,500 in sales for a total reward of $7,550. How would that affect your productivity for that last week of June? I don't know about your sales team, but $1,510 extra provides a great incentive to hit expectations. Play out the same math for achieving the goal standards and the incentive increases dramatically. Could you make an additional four and a half sales to get that 4% bonus for achieving the goal? I know I sure as heck would give it my best effort by following up with every opportunity I could. Add in recognition rewards like trophies, names on a plaque, gift cards, cash bonuses, T-shirts, etc. and you turn your "jet fuel" into "rocket fuel." Using this type of strategy will get the most out of your sales team's potential and play a big part in the environment of your Culture.

Guess what happens now? It all starts over next month. With this type of strategy, we aren't increasing the bar each month based on the results of last month, we are just resetting the starting point.

Ok team—great month! Let's do it again next month!

Helpful Hints
The shorter the time frame for our incentive, the more we involve the strategy of "instant gratification" to our program. Studies have proven time and time again that people will take a smaller reward now over a bigger reward in the future. Ever heard the saying, "A bird in hand, is worth more than two in the bush"? Once again, it comes down to basic human behavior. I can have it now or maybe get something bigger in the future if I wait. Give it to me now! Knowing I can get something now or very soon over possibly getting something in the future is a huge motivating factor when it comes to incentive.

Key Point: The more we apply the strategy of recognition and award over cash reward when it comes to bonuses and achievement, the more someone will associate that recognition or award with your business and how much you care for them. Here's a quick example to prove my point. Give someone $100 for achieving a goal, and they will spend it in a multitude of places, associating none of the things they purchased with you or your company. Give someone two baseball tickets to see their favorite team with their wife or friend, and they work for the greatest company on the planet.

I will share more about these incentivizing concepts at the end of the chapter when I get into the bonus material on contests to drive sales. (See what I did there?)

A Note on Incentive
Incentive is probably another subject I could write a book about, but there is already a pretty good one out there called Freakonomics by Steven Levitt and Stephen Dubner. Reading that book changed the way I approached getting a desired result out of a team or individual. It is well worth

reading if you don't see the value or understand the pros and cons of applying incentives. You would be surprised how often we think we are applying the right incentive to get the desired result, and it actually ends up backfiring on us and getting the opposite effect. ***Key Point:*** If you ever catch yourself wondering why people aren't doing what you want them to do—or worse, doing the opposite—you can bet that your incentive is all wrong.

What will your strategy be to incentivize your team to reach their potential using your commission structure?

How will you hold them accountable to your commission structure?

WRITE IT DOWN!

Step 3: Setting Activity Standards for Sales Accountability (KPI's)

Alright, we have a strategy for how much we want our sales team to sell and how we will reward them when they do, but how will they achieve these standards? It all comes down to the activities they need to perform and how many they need to bring about the desired results. These activities indicate the level of performance necessary of our team to achieve the desired standards. These activities are called Key Performance Indicators, or KPI's for short.

What we have to ask ourselves is, "What are the key activities our sales team needs to perform that will bring about the desired result of achieving our standards?"

The best way I have found to determine these activities is to work it backwards from the desired result. I suggest doing so from the productivity expectations you have set for the team. In our example exercise below, we will round up to the next nearest half a point to keep it simple and guarantee success. Do not round down, or your KPI's will be too low.

In our Step 1 example for setting production standards for a sales team, we determined that our monthly expectation (or the result we desired) was $75,000. We also determined that our first KPI for our sales team—the number of jobs one needs to sell in order to achieve expectations—is 7.5, based on our average sale of $10,000. (See Figure 6.1)

Sales/Wins	Result
7.5	$75,000

Figure 6.1

Taking into consideration that you need to win 7.5 jobs in order to achieve expectations, how many estimates will you have to give to achieve that number of jobs? Well, that depends on what your company averages. Do 50% of your estimates turn into jobs you win? 30%? 20%? Oh Lord... 10%? Whatever that number is for your specific situation, that is the number you need to use in order to set the appropriate standard for your team's activity. Let's use 20% for our example. At a rate of 20% of our estimates turn into sales/wins, we would have to give 37.5 estimates a month to achieve expectations. (See Figure 6.2)

Estimates	Sales/Wins	Result
37.5	7.5	$75,000

Figure 6.2

Let's continue. How many presentations would you have to do to deliver 37.5 estimates per month? Well, what percentage of your presentations afford you the opportunity to estimate the job? 100%? 90%? 70%? Please, God no! 50%? Whatever that number is for you, it is your performance standard, or indicator. Let's use 70% for our example. At a rate of 70% of our presentations turning into a delivered estimate, we would have to give approximately 54 presentations per month to achieve our standard for expectations. (See Figure 6.3)

Presentations	Estimates	Sales/Wins	Result
54	37.5	7.5	$75,000

Figure 6.3

Now that you get the idea, what are the KPI's for your sales team in your particular situation? What terminology do you use? The following are some of the common KPI's and terminology we see when working with our clients here at Contractor Coach PRO:

The expected result
- Result
- Revenue
- Gross Sales Volume (GSV)

The total number of sales or jobs needed to achieve the expected result
- Wins
- Sales
- Contracts
- Jobs

The total number of offers to retain your service or buy your product needed in order to achieve the expected number of sales

- Estimates
- Proposals
- Bids

The total number of prospective customers needed to present your product or service to in order to achieve the expected number of estimates or sales

- Presentations
- Demos
- Sits

The total number of prospective customers that actually need and are interested in your product or service to achieve the expected number of opportunities, presentations, or estimates

- Prospects
- Opportunities

The total number of inspections needed to achieve the expected # of opportunities, presentations, or estimates

- Inspections
- Assessments

The total number of either onsite or online meetings to perform an inspection or present your products—including no-shows—needed to achieve the expected number of inspections

- Appointments

The total number of prospective customers who requested or showed interest needed to achieve

the expected number of either an appointment or inspection
- Leads
- Call-Ins

The total number of prospective customers you need to actually contact to achieve the expected number of leads, appointments, inspections, or opportunities
- Contacts
- Interactions
- Contacted

The total number of attempts at direct interaction with a prospective customer, usually by phone or knocking on their door, needed to achieve the expected number of contacts, leads, or appointments
- Attempts
- Calls
- Cold Calls
- Door Knocks

The total number of attempts made to market yourself without specifically presenting on an appointment needed to achieve the expected number of contacts, leads, or appointments. (This normally relates to marketing through various types of print or social media. For example, if I put out 50 flyers, got 22 likes on a Facebook post, handed out 12 brochures at a networking event, and dropped off 5 business cards, my total impressions would be 89.)
- Impressions
- Likes
- Flyers
- Business Cards

This is by no means an all-inclusive list. Different clients, in different markets, with different products and Processes have varying KPI's. The key to being successful in developing yours is to understand the various key stages that your Process goes through and how each of those key stages should indicate the ultimate success of the next stage. Here is an example of what it might look like in the end, using the numbers we started with before (See Figure 6.4):

Leads	Appts.	Inspect	Opp.	Demos	Estimates	Wins	Result
125	90	80	60	54	37.5	7.5	$75,000

Figure 6.4

By setting standards for our KPI's, we develop an expectation of the level of activity it takes to achieve the expected standards of productivity that we determined earlier. When we track these KPI's, we now have an opportunity to see where a specific teammate is deficient, and we also have a visual representation of why they are or are not achieving expectations. Unfortunately, with most home services contractors, the only thing we have to go off of is the result because there are no standards for activity. If the result we are looking for is where we need it to be, that specific rep is "good." If the result is not up to our expectations, the only thing we can assume is that the specific rep is "lazy." The reality is that in most cases the rep is not lazy; they are deficient in the execution of one or more of the KPI's. If we know which ones those are, we can apply the appropriate coaching for that activity, and, funny enough, their results will likely improve dramatically.

Tracking your team's KPI's is another area of your strategy where you can start simple and improve as your business grows. I suggest determining the most important KPI's to the success of a teammate. For example, in sales you might start with leads, appointments, demos, and wins to measure the activity you need to achieve your expected result. If a teammate's level of activity is what is needed to achieve the expected result, but the result isn't happening, consider adding to your KPI's to determine where the teammate might be deficient in their activity.

Measuring

As we discussed before, accountability is setting a standard and being held accountable to that standard. We have set several standards at this point in the chapter, and in doing so you should understand the strategy for setting standards. You should be able to take this knowledge and set additional standards for each teammate in your business.

You may be thinking that this setting standards thing is all good and fine, but how do you hold people accountable to them? With the most important of the 7 Leadership Habits, of course: inspect what we expect. We do this by measuring the productivity and activity of our team as it compares to the expected result and then reviewing those results with each teammate.

First, we need a strategy to measure our standards. Fortunately, with a lot of the technology available out there today, gathering the necessary information is fairly easy. When used properly, many of the CRM's available today can help with your KPI's. We can get data on the number of leads, appointments, opportunities, estimates, wins, and revenue in most CRM's with some even providing more information. Unfortunately, this isn't all the information we need in most cases, so it is hard to get a valuable KPI report within our CRM. Fortunately, you can download that data into a spreadsheet, add the columns for the activities you want to track, and source the rest of the data manually from other tools and the file itself. This will give you the insight you need to review and coach your team.

Maybe some of you out there haven't hopped on the technology train yet by using a CRM to manage the data on your customers. My next book will feature a chapter on Technology, in which I hope to convince you of its value. Until then, when it comes to measuring standards, spreadsheets are your friend. If you aren't a spreadsheet wizard, don't worry, everything we have covered in this book is pretty simple to manage with basic spreadsheet ability. If spreadsheets just aren't your thing, and you don't want them to be your thing, either find a Spreadsheet Champion or you can always fall back on the old school way of doing things on whiteboards or pen and paper. No matter what your proficiency is with technology, tracking your standards is an absolute must in growing and scaling your business.

If you want to make your life easier in tracking your standards and KPI's, I strongly recommend hopping on with one of our coaches to help you resolve the problem and make your life easier. We not only have all of the templates we discussed and dozens more, but we help brand and customize them for you and coach you in a way that you learn how to use them and have the knowledge to do it for others in the future. Yep, we literally coach ourselves out of a job. Fortunately, there are a lot of you to help.

Reviews

I cannot stress enough the importance of doing reviews with everyone on your team to assess their performance, give coaching, and develop an action plan to improve. Even our best teammates always have room to improve.

A review isn't just about the numbers—it's about all of the standards that you hold your team accountable to. Your culture and their behavior, productivity, activity, and—most importantly—how they are progressing in your company and toward their Dreams. In other words, reviews assess how a teammate is progressing toward being a leader in your company while helping their leader improve as well.

When doing reviews, we suggest the following strategy.

Step 1: Develop a Review Scorecard
This chapter has been all about setting standards and being accountable to those standards. The review scorecard is a culmination of that accountability. Not just how accountable a specific teammate is, but the accountability of their direct reporting authority, their department, and the company as a whole to the standards that have been set. *Key Point:* The number one reason why managers and owners don't do reviews is because they are also held accountable in the review—if they are doing reviews correctly.

I still remember getting my own coaching from a trusted mentor when it came to reviews. They explained to me that I needed to develop a review scorecard to hold the team accountable to our standards, just as I am coaching you here. I can remember thinking to myself, "That's no big deal. I can do that," right up until they said I needed to include an area in the scorecard for each teammate to score me. "Uh oh," I thought. "How would my team score me?" I can assure you that if that is your first thought as you hear this, then you too have room for improvement. Embrace that! Encourage that in your team! If you are going to be a great leader, who better to get constructive feedback from than those who you are currently leading? Nothing improved my own leadership more than allowing my team to score my performance, the performance of our leaders, and the performance of our company overall.

Here is what you should include for your scorecard:
- Name of Reviewee
- Their Position of Role
- Date of the Review
- Performance according to the Quota, Expectations, and Goal of their position
- A (1-10) score for each of the skills for the position they hold
- An (1-10) overall Culture score
- A (+/- or = to our expectations) score for each of your Core Values
- Their KPI's Scorecard since the last review
- Their score for you in the following areas:
    - Overall leadership (+/- or = to what they expect)
    - Your ability to Connect (+/- or = to what they expect)
    - A score for each of the 7 Leadership Habits (1-10)
    - Overall example of the company's Core Values (+/- or = to what they expect)
    - Overall example of the company's Purpose (+/- or = to what they expect)

Next, we want to include some observation and feedback in our scorecard by asking:
- What do you think we have done well over the (past week/month/quarter/year—based on how often you plan to review)?
- What do you think we have done well over the past (amount of time between reviews)?
- What areas could you improve to be more effective?
- These are the areas we see that would move you closer to your dreams and aspirations.
- What areas could we improve to be more effective?

- What, if any, concerns do you have when being a part of our team?

Step 2: Develop an Improvement Action Plan
Based on the discussion and scores, as well as the performance based on the KPI report, there should be some easily identifiable areas for improvement. The idea is to agree on two to three goals to improve their overall performance between now and their next review. Once those goals are agreed upon, we want to write up an action plan so we can measure their progress in achieving those goals by the end of the upcoming review period. Your action plan should include:

- Goal
- Two to three Action Steps
- Start and End Dates for each Action
- Any Tools or Resources Required
- Desired Outcome of Each Action
- An Area for Notes to Clarify and Update the Action as it Progresses
- A Completion Score for the Next Review (EE: Exceeded Expectations; AE: Achieved Expectations; FM: Failed to Meet Expectations)

Last but not least, have a signature at the bottom of your scorecard for both the teammate and the reporting authority giving the review. Signing the review scorecard indicates an agreement that the scorecard is accurate and that each party agrees to the Action Plan.

Some final comments on accountability... Carefully consider all the standards you set. They must be achievable while still pushing your team members to reach their potential. If you make them too hard to achieve, you run the risk of firing everyone who doesn't meet them. If you make them too easy, your team members won't feel challenged and will end up seeking another opportunity where they will be. Even worse, by not setting your standards high enough, you allow for average or below average people to be a member of your team. Those types of people will eventually feel entitled and never leave! ***Key Point:*** A good rule of thumb is if you haven't, wouldn't, or couldn't achieve the standards you have set, why would you expect anyone who isn't financially invested into your business to do so? No one will ever treat your business like you do until they are financially invested in it like you are, and even then, they still may not treat it as you do if they haven't gone through what you have prior to that investment. When setting standards, expect 75-80% of the effort you would put in, and you'll be realistic about setting standards that can be achieved. There simply isn't anything like the responsibility of owning a business and the 100%+ amount of effort it takes to make it successful.

Remember, when you are establishing your standards, you are a person of your word, and your reputation is too important not to hold people accountable to the standards you have set. These standards will determine who works for you and who doesn't. If you don't hold your teammates to them, they are meaningless, and you don't really have standards.

"Iron sharpens iron, and one person sharpens another."
—Proverbs 27:17

Bonus Content!
Contests and Bonuses

When I originally sat down to write this book, I did not include contests and bonuses, but after sharing so much about incentive, I wanted to add a little more rocket fuel to your strategy.

When I first learned about the power of incentives, I decided that I wanted to get more out of my team by heavily incentivizing them. I wanted them to give it their all in an effort to help them realize their full potential. My company was like a lab; I tested every way possible to get the most out of my team. Most of those efforts were huge failures that either cost us more than what we had allotted in our budget or fell flat because the incentive didn't match the effort. Some efforts ended up having an even more dramatic effect and made team members less invested. I hope this bonus content helps you avoid some of those same mistakes.

First, any time you are working on something to incentivize your team, ask yourself these four things:
1. Is it in the budget, and is it worth giving up that piece of the pie?
2. What would you do if you were in their shoes?
3. What effect will this incentive have if we implement it?
4. Who will this new incentive motivate?

Just asking these four questions will help you avoid a lot of issues.

Rule #1 for a great contest or bonus program is that there is no "winner" or even a 1st, 2nd, or 3rd prize. I know... How is it a contest if there is no winner? I continue to see these types of incentive programs throughout our industry, and while they do motivate, they only motivate a select few and rarely move the needle much in the big scheme of things.

Think about it. When you run this type of contest, who wins? It is almost always the same two or three teammates. Super motivating for them, but absolutely no interest for the rest of the team. It usually goes like this...

You announce your brilliant new contest and the prizes, trophies, and rewards for the winners. Everyone seems pumped and excited, including you. Literally the next day, your top sales rep—let's call him Dan—starts announcing all the new leads, inspections, appointments, sales, referrals, or whatever the contest is about, and how he is not only killing it with [insert absurdly high number here], but he has [insert another absurdly high number here] in the pipeline before the week is out. Now, that might motivate your other top sales rep—let's call him Jim (the silent killer type that doesn't announce their number till the final day of the contest, usually shattering anything Dan actually turns in)—but what effect does it have on the rest of the team?

Here's what's running through their mind: "Geez, Dan is already killing it. I don't have anywhere close to that number, and I sure don't have that in my pipeline. Jim sure is being quiet... I bet he's got a ton too. I haven't seen him in the office much lately, and he always wins. I guess this is just another contest I don't have a chance at."

Sure enough, as the sun sets on the final day of the contest, Jim wins, Dan comes in second, and they both receive all the recognition, high fives, trophies, and—most importantly—the reward. Meanwhile, everyone else on the team is getting a little tired of not winning and going unnoticed. Every contest they lose a little more incentive to push themselves to their potential.

On the other hand, you have an opportunity to create another powerful moment here with a truly brilliant contest. What if everyone could win? I know what you are thinking. "Well, if everyone can win, then that's not really a contest, is it?" I know because I used to think that as well, and you are absolutely wrong—just like I was. It is the most productive contest you will ever run.

What if, instead of saying the top dog—or even top two to three dogs—win, we were to say that everyone who achieves this [insert achievable but motivating number here] wins? How does that change the thinking of the entire team? First off, Dan and Jim will still be at each other's throats to win because it's all about the competition and recognition for them. You will likely get similar results from your top people, but everyone else isn't being compared to those guys. They are being compared to—you guessed it—a standard! Dan and Jim can go off and set all kinds of records never achieved before, but they still have incentive to meet the goal. How much different do you think the overall result of your contest will be? From the experience I had as a contractor and the results of contractors we have coached over the last seven years, you can expect about a 30-40% improvement in the total results of your contest! You can also expect a much happier team that loves being pushed by your brilliant contests. Best of all, you get to recognize a lot more people who achieved the goal, and there is nothing people like more than being recognized for their value!

Funny enough, one of the places I consistently see business owners implement the "everybody can win" strategy is in longer contests or bonuses programs. For example, there's a company vacation on the line for everyone who sells $1 million in gross sales this year. Sure enough, over half of the sales teams consistently go on those trips. I still haven't figured out why they haven't applied that same logic to shorter incentives.

Now that we have the ground rules for how to run contests and bonus programs, let's talk about when, how long, and for what?

Our advice is that if you need a spike in some area of your sales pipeline, more leads, appointments, inspections, contracts, orders, or even more collections, it's time to run a short-term contest. When I say "short-term," I mean a week or two and no longer than a month. If you need a spike in more than one area, make it a combo contest.

Here's an example. I am checking my numbers and looking at reports. I talk with my production team and notice there is a down tick in leads, and we are running short on orders to keep our production staff busy. Time for a Combo Meal! With a little investigation into our numbers, I determined that we need 200 fresh leads to refill our pipeline and 40 new jobs to keep our production team at full bore. We need to generate those numbers over a two-week time period. I have 10 reps on my sales team that are currently generating 50 new leads per week and 10 new orders. I have to insert some incentive to double our current production over the next two weeks in both of those areas of our sales process, and I don't want to just barely make it.

This is what my contest would look like...

> "Hey everybody, we need your help. First, we need to keep your pipeline so full that you continue to make great money by pushing to increase your self-generated leads more than we have been. Don't worry, we will continue to market and generate company leads. Second, we need to generate enough

new orders to keep our two-week backlog of work. This helps our production team to keep working so we don't lose anyone. You all know those guys are rockstars and hard to find!

In order to help you achieve the goals of the contest, I will be running some intensive training sessions throughout the contest to keep you sharp. You can also expect me to play my part by getting out there in the field with you for some hand-to-hand combat coaching!

Additionally, you can also expect our support team to be there to help you process your orders quickly to ensure they get in on time.

So, here's our mission! We need to create 200 new self-generated leads and 40 new orders in the next two weeks.

Everyone that generates on average 15 new leads and three new orders per week for the next two weeks will get [an incentive that is financially appropriate and fits the environment of our culture]. They have to be verifiable new leads, generated starting today, and entered into our CRM by 5pm two weeks from now. The orders must be turned in, submitted for approval, and approved for production by 5pm two weeks from now. Any orders currently turned in or submitted are not included in the contest. I know this is a tall order, but I have no doubt that we have the talent on this team to have everyone achieve these goals! Are there any questions about the contest?"

So, let's break it down.

10 reps current two-week production = 100 new leads and 20 new orders

We need 200 new leads and 40 new orders to keep our pipelines full. If each rep hits the goals of the contest, we will have 300 new leads and 60 new orders, a third again more than we need!

Why would I set the goals for the contest at more than we need? There are several reasons, but the most important is that I know for a fact that not everyone will win the contest. Our studies have shown that instead of the "top dog/1st, 2nd, 3rd" approach to a contest, which only has 20% of the team hit the goal, our "everybody can win" approach has 50% of the team achieve the goal, resulting in 150 new self-generated leads and 30 new orders. The other 50% of the team will make up the remainder of what we need if they simply keep up their previous production. Our research has shown that even though they may not achieve the goal of the contest, their production does rise by about 30% during the time of the contest.

The key to a short contest like this is to keep it top of mind with daily engagement, education, empathy, encouragement, empowerment, and the expectation that everyone will win. Those 7 Leadership Habits come in handy again. Most of all, set the example by getting in the trenches if necessary to show that you aren't expecting them to do anything you wouldn't do yourself. Get a group chat going regarding everyone's progress. Run an engaging training. Pay special attention to the reps that aren't on pace and spend time in the field with them. Celebrate each time someone succeeds. Allow your top reps to take an underperformer under their wing. Don't make exceptions for who qualifies and who doesn't by being clear with the rules of your contest and holding yourself and everyone else accountable to them.

For these shorter contests, be careful not to run them every week. By having various contests based on what you need, you avoid a lot of possible sandbagging by your team, but if you get into a pattern or do them too often you leave the possibility of the more clever teammates sandbagging. You also run the risk of a roller coaster effect by having a contest one week and then not one the next over and over. Be inconsistently consistent with your short-term, needs-based contests.

For longer contests (like hitting the expectation and goal each month), you can add a little cherry on top with some cash incentives. X for reaching the expectation and Y for achieving the goal. It still allows everyone to win according to your standards. As I said before, I am not a fan of cash incentives and their value to the business, but sometimes the value of money given to the individual should be considered. Hitting expectations and goals is a good place to use a cash bonus incentive.

Be creative with your contests, have fun with them, make sure the rules are clear, and don't allow for loopholes. Most importantly of all is to be the Contest Champion!

I will leave you with my favorite style of contest. This is a mid-length contest, at least a month long but no more than four months. It involves a weighted point system for all the activities on the KPI scorecard and creates friendly competition that drives the team for a "season." Think of it as Fantasy Football for home services contractors.

Here is the general idea: you have a team of sales reps, each of those reps is an individual "team" that will play another "team" based on a predetermined schedule each week of the "season." If you have a large team of reps, you will want to divide them into "divisions" and possibly "leagues" if your company is really large. Each rep's team scores points based on their activities on their KPI scorecard for that week of the "season" to determine the winner for that week's "game." If we use the final KPI example we created earlier, it might look something like this:

Point Values

Leads	Appts.	Inspect	Opp.	Demos	Estimates	Wins
1 pt	2 pts	3 pts	4 pts	6 pts	7 pts	10 pts

Each KPI score is based on its value of achieving that activity. For example, it would take 10 inspections to equal just three wins. Both are worth a total of 30 points. A team's final score for a week might look something like this:

Weekly Result

Leads	Appts.	Inspect	Opp.	Demos	Estimates	Wins	Score
10	5	4	3	3	3	1	
10 pts	10 pts	12 pts	12 pts	18 pts	21 pts	10 pts	93

Upon completion of a season, you tally up the wins and losses and proceed to a two to four week "playoff season" to determine your "Super Bowl of Sales" Championship and eventual winner. This type of contest can be a lot of fun when the sales team is really into it. That will be determined by how big of a Contest Champion you or someone on your team is. The teammates will create super cool and likely very funny team names. They will have side bets. There will be stunning victories and agonizing losses, and you will find the entire company tuning in weekly to see the results. Have a huge ridiculous championship trophy or belt and killer rewards for weekly high points, division and league winners, and records for KPI scores both total and by activity. Of course, the Champ gets more than a trophy or belt, making it special. Do this right, and it will be the highest grossing quarter of your year, every year.

Be great!

The Last Word

When I began to write this book, the plan was to include all 12 strategies of *The Contractor's Blueprint*. As I sat on a mountain top in northern New Mexico, praying and meditating each morning for God's guidance, writing and rewriting, contemplating and organizing, editing and rethinking, it started to become painfully obvious that one book could not do justice to what I want to share with home services contractors everywhere. Did you know that the average best-selling book is 50,000 words? Me neither 'til I looked it up, because I was at 40,000 words on day five! As I type this sentence, it puts this book over 50,000 words after a lot of editing. Now, by no means do I believe this is a best seller—the thought makes me laugh—but it does give me an indication of how long a book should be if I want someone to read it. So here I sit, my main goal to write a book to empower others has been accomplished, but I still feel like there is unfinished business. What do they say about when we make a plan? "God laughs." He is probably rolling around up there in the heavens right now as I'm typing this sentence.

I am not the type to want to do things halfway and just throw something out there. So, I had to make a decision; do I just keep everything high level and hope it's enough, or should I write two books and spend the time to do it right with the Foundational DNA to start helping contractors sooner rather than later? Then, in the near future complete the set with a book on the Operational DNA? As you know by now, I chose the latter option, and I believe it ended up being for the best. I give you my word that the second book will be out before you can accomplish everything I've shared in this book. Maybe that was His plan all along.

What I hope to have given you in this first book is the strategic blueprint to set a strong foundation for your company and the relationship that each of your Foundational DNA strategies have with the others. I want you to know how key it is to get the order right for your business, and how having the right strategy for your specific situation can cause radical improvements in your ability to start working on your business instead of in it. I also hope that I made you stop long enough to think about your Leadership, Culture, Processes, Organization, Finances, and Accountability strategies of your business, yourself, and the impact they will have on others. Most of all, I hope you paused long enough to really consider your purpose and why you're doing what you are doing in this place at this time. I hope this book has made you realize your ability to impact the world around you and the legacy you will leave behind one day. I genuinely pray that it is an epic one because it fulfills who you are.

If you take the time to get these Foundational DNA strategies right, they will have a massive impact on the success of your Operational DNA strategies for Technology, Marketing, Sales, Production, Training, and Recruiting, Hiring & Onboarding (RHO) that will be in the second book.

Finally, I hope that particular aspects of this book had an impact on you. There are three big concepts: connection, capacity, and aligning your purpose to avoid an identity gap between who you are and why you are doing what you are doing. I wanted to make sure you didn't miss them.

First, that you really consider how you will *connect* with others and how key it is, as your Super Skill, to get people to buy-in, be active and disciplined, and get results, with the end result being trust, respect, and ultimately belief in you as a leader. Remember your team wants to connect with you, so reciprocating that energy will be a win-win. When I say "connect," I don't mean through social media, phone calls, texts, and emails. While these all are valuable means of communication, true connection comes from direct interaction and forming a relationship with one another. Connections are two-way streets. Each person in that relationship genuinely wants the best for the other and cares enough to help them get there.

Second, that you see the importance of creating more *capacity* to work on your business instead of in it. As you gain more capacity, you are able to realize your dreams and goals sooner, affording you more opportunity at an even more epic impact. To do so, you will have to first become a great leader and then identify and grow the Champions you will need to make that impact. Don't forget to automate, eliminate, and delegate as many of your duties and business responsibilities that you are weak at as possible.

Finally, there is more to all of this than just your business. It's really about your life, fulfilling who you are, and aligning that with the *purpose* you want to achieve. Hopefully, that purpose has an epic impact far beyond you and into the future as a legacy of who you are and why you existed. A piece of you that others will learn from, carry on, and hopefully improve on, to serve others for years to come.

You have to *connect* to gain the *capacity* to achieve your ultimate *purpose*. When you achieve your ultimate purpose, I pray you find joy in fulfilling your version of success.

A Little Guidance

If you're anything like me, when I get a book like this, I have the tendency to read through it first and then go back and use the golden nuggets that I think I need to add to my business or knowledge. If that is the case for you, I hope you found something useful to make your business and your life a little easier. If the book is really good, I go back to the beginning, really dig into each exercise, and execute them to the best of my ability, step-by-step until I am done. There have been books that have helped me with my business and life that took me a year or more to implement, but they were absolutely worth the effort. I hope this is one of those for you.

Now, whether you are the type to go back and do it all like me, or you are the exceptional breed that implements as you read, stopping at each step to develop your strategies and tactics for the foundation of your business, then you probably will meet obstacles and struggles along the way. There will be areas and concepts you didn't completely understand, there will be things you only get partially done, and there will be strategies you just didn't develop because you didn't know where to start. All of this allows the enemy of your absolute belief—doubt—to creep in. First off, if any of this happened for you, please let me know where I could improve the book to make it easier to follow for future readers (you can find my email address in the Resources Section in the back of this book). Additionally, if you have any questions that will help clarify an area that you are struggling with, shoot me an email and I will do my best to answer.

Last but not least, if you really want to take control of your business so it can grow and you can achieve freedom, and if following the instructions of a book just aren't your thing, but you saw the value in the contents of this book, take our Contractor Strategy Assessment (you can find the link in the resources section). Set up a time with one of our coaches for a free strategy call. If we are a match—great. If not, I assure you, that strategy call will get you headed in the right direction.

Okay, that is enough about the book and how we might help you achieve your dreams. I want to leave you with a little wisdom. A little is all I have. First, things aren't important, people are, and...

"If you care enough to willingly serve others, they will know that you love them."

This is how we at Contractor Coach PRO see our Core Values: to Love, Serve, and Care. By living these core values every day, we define who we are and how we believe others should be treated. I believe that several of the problems we face in the world today could be resolved by putting others first. It took me a long time to understand this, and I want you to seriously consider how you're approaching business and life. If you are in search of peace and happiness, living your life this way could go a long way to helping you find it.

I will leave you with my favorite verse...

"Finally, brothers and sisters, whatever is true, whatever is worthy of respect, whatever is just, whatever is pure, whatever is lovely, whatever is commendable, if something is excellent or worthy of praise, think on these things."
—Philippians 4:8

A winning strategy is all about outthinking everyone else…

…and then executing.

Resources

- Facebook Group: Contractor Community | Control, Growth and Freedom for Contractors
- Book Website: https://www.contractorsblueprintbook.com
- Coaching Website: https://www.contractorcoachpro.com/
- Contractor Assessment: https://s.surveyanyplace.com/ccpassessment
- Contractor's Training Room: https://www.contractorcoachpro.com/contractor-training-room/
- Contractor Radio Podcast: https://contractorcoachpro.com/podcast/
- TOP REP High Performance Sales Training: https://topreptraining.com/
- Contractor Boost - From 6 Figure Contractor to 7 Figure Business: https://contractorcoachpro.com/boost/
- Breaking Dreams Youtube Video - https://www.youtube.com/watch?v=amGCaoO3MTk

Leadership Reading

1. John C. Maxwell
   - *Developing the Leader Within You*
   - *Leadership 101: What Every Leader Needs to Know*
   - *Leadershift: The 11 Essential Changes Every Leader Must Embrace*
   - *Everyone Communicates, Few Connect: What the Most Effective People Do Differently*
   - *Good Leaders Ask Great Questions: Your Foundation for Successful Leadership*

2. Ken Blanchard
   - *The One Minute Manager*
   - *Lead Like Jesus*
   - *The Secret: What Great Leaders Know and Do*
   - *The Heart of a Leader: Insights on the Art of Influence*
3. Stephen Covey
   - *The 7 Habits of Highly Effective People (these are different than the 7 Leadership Habits from this book)*
   - *Principle-Centered Leadership*
   - *Daniel Pink*
   - *Drive*
4. Simon Sinek
   - *Leaders Eat Last: Why Some Teams Pull Together and Others Don't*

Culture Reading

1. Simon Sinek
   - *Start With Why: How Great Leaders Inspire Everyone to Take Action*
2. Robert Glazer
   - *Elevate: Push Beyond Your Limits and Unlock Success in Yourself and Others*
3. Laszlo Bock
   - *Work Rules!: Insights from Inside Google that Will Transform How You Live and Lead*

Incentive Reading

1. Steven Levitt/Stephen Dubner
   - *Freakonomics: A Rogue Economist Explores the Hidden Side of Everything*

Acknowledgments

This book is dedicated to my grandfather, Pappy. It was his insight into who I was and why I do what I do that led me down a path to begin coaching contractors. I wouldn't be here today, doing what I am doing, without him. The example he set for me on how to approach life by being a man of my word in service to others is something I will never be able to repay, except by paying it forward.

I can't mention any endeavor I have taken on for the past 28 years without mentioning my wife, Michelle, who has always supported, encouraged, and grounded me as I chase my dreams in business and in life. I couldn't be more thankful that God put her in my life. She has truly made me a better person. Without her, I would likely be buried in a desert somewhere by now.

I want to thank my team, Nathan, Braden, Jenny, Rosalyn, Jon, Chuck, Jordan, Paul, and Arp, for encouraging me and supporting me to take the time to write this book. They believed that there was something here that needed to be written and shared with the world. Their ability to challenge me on the concepts and content of the book made all the difference. In particular, I want to thank Nathan. His ability to ask great questions and provide valuable insight was paramount to the success of this book. I wish everyone could have a team like ours!

There would be no *Contractor's Blueprint* without Zac Kerr, who was the first to say I should write a book about the blueprint after speaking at one of our Contractor Strategy Conferences. I am eternally grateful, not just for the encouragement, but for his insight as a great leader, for the forward he wrote, and—most of all—for his friendship.

I also want to thank all the industry leaders, experts, mentors, and friends who took time to read the book before publishing it and offered excellent feedback and suggestions to make it even better. I especially want to thank Jory Allen, John Dye, Derik Kline, Tom Self, Adam Buttorff, Vance Garvey, Ryan Shantz, Matthew Danskin, and Matt Grassmeyer. This list would not be complete without my amazing friend and Details Champion, Matthew Morrisson! I first met Matthew nine years ago when I was selling software, and he was implementing it for the contractor he was working for. I have never met someone with more questions, suggestions and an ability to break things and make them better. He did such a great job with implementing the software that he got fired. I immediately knew we needed to hire him. It would no doubt make our software better. We did, he has, and he continues to fluster the Idealist in me to this day because I understand the value of our friendship. He has made me a better person and this book a better book by bombarding me with questions, suggestions, and explanations as to why something didn't make sense. Thanks, Matthew, for always being thoughtful in your questions—even if they are annoying sometimes. I love you for it!

No acknowledgement would be complete without thanking the contractors and vendors throughout the contracting world who have championed Contractor Coach PRO and *The Contractor's Blueprint*! The support has been humbling, and we will continue to Love, Serve, and Care for you all.

Last but certainly not least, I want to thank all of our community and clients here at Contractor Coach PRO. This is your book. Without you, I would never have realized how it all fit together or all the strategies we needed to consider to create a business that we can be proud of. These last eight years have been an amazing journey with you all. I will always be grateful for your contributions to this book and how we coach. With you, we will continue to get better every day!

www.ingramcontent.com/pod-product-compliance
Lightning Source LLC
Chambersburg PA
CBHW042120190326
41519CB00031B/7558